WILLIAM HAZLITT

Selected Essays

Crofts Classics

WILLIAM HAZLITT

Selected
Essays

EDITED BY

John R. Nabholtz

LOYOLA UNIVERSITY (CHICAGO)

APPLETON-CENTURY-CROFTS

Educational Division

New York MEREDITH CORPORATION

659–1

Library of Congress Card Number: 70–91403

PRINTED IN THE UNITED STATES OF AMERICA

390–22591–6

contents

introduction

A characteristic procedure of the personal essays that William Hazlitt wrote in his final years is the examination of his past and the assertion of the continuity of his moral character and experience. Although the search for the grounds of the authentic self was a frequent preoccupation of the writers of his generation and constituted a prevailing form of literary expression, the self-evaluation that Hazlitt conducted cannot be explained simply as a matter of literary fashion; it was the necessary response to the demands of a complex personal history. Hazlitt's life had more than its share of sensation and drama; he was the perennial outsider and vigorous protester against the established social and political order, and for extended periods the subject of public controversy and scandal. His literary production was not only enormous, but astonishingly diverse, embracing biography, theatrical criticism, essays and books on politics, literature, painting, and philosophy, as well as a long series of familiar essays. That Hazlitt in his last years should look for the continuity in his personal and intellectual life was therefore singularly appropriate, and it suggests the path to be followed by the student of his life and works.

Repeatedly in his valedictory essays, Hazlitt returns in memory to the stirring events of the final decade of the eighteenth century; and he takes pride in the fact that he remained true to the energies and ideals of that revolutionary time. As he so clearly recognized, the decade of the 1790's was the seminal period and the moral testing ground for himself and his generation. "It was the dawn of a new era," he recalls in 1827; "a new impulse had been given to men's minds, and the sun of Liberty rose upon the sun of Life in the same day, and both were proud to run their race together." Throughout his life he was to judge his society, its politics, its art, and the intellectual and moral character of its most representative figures in terms of their

fidelity to the golden promise of human freedom repre-
sented by the French Revolution and to the personal aspirations that accompanied it.

In Hazlitt's own case, the final decade of the eighteenth
century meant not only the fulfillment of the political
hopes of the dissenting tradition in which he was nur-
tured, but it also signified the period in which he initiated
the personal associations and intellectual preoccupations
that shaped the rest of his life. Between 1792 and 1800,
he became acquainted with the leading literary figures of
the day, Wordsworth and Coleridge; he began his lifelong
involvement with the pictorial arts; and, perhaps most important for his reputation and influence in English literature, he embarked on an intensive study of "modern philosophy" and struggled to formulate his own philosophy of
the mind and its dealings with experience.

These philosophic investigations finally found expression
in An Essay on the Principles of Human Action (1805),
Hazlitt's first publication, and one he always regarded as
of paramount importance for the metaphysical "discovery"
it contained. As a student of eighteenth-century empirical
philosophy in the tradition of John Locke, Hazlitt is
wholeheartedly committed to the premise that the sensa-
tions of pleasure and pain lodged in the mind by concrete and particular experience are the ultimate basis of
human knowledge. However, he takes sharp issue with
those philosophers in the empirical tradition who concluded that the mind is necessarily mechanical and selfish
in its formulation and evaluation of sense impressions.
In reply to these charges, Hazlitt argues that the mind is
not "the mere puppet of matter," but possesses a super-
intending faculty, the imagination, that can combine, order, and modify the manifold impressions of experience in
terms of uniquely human values and aspirations. The imagination can create ideas or "images" of the good and the
pleasurable, for the possession and enjoyment of which
the will is stirred into activity. Furthermore, through the
imagination the individual mind is propelled outside of
itself and its own concerns into sympathetic identification
with the good or the pleasurable as it exists in or for
another.

In the Essay of 1805, Hazlitt is primarily concerned

with the imagination as an ethical faculty, as proof of the "benevolence" of the human mind and in answer to those political writers and philosophers who oppose the democratic impulses of the age because of their belief in the essential selfishness of human nature. However, it was in relation to aesthetics and the psychology of the artistic process that Hazlitt's theory of the creative and sympathetic powers of the mind was to receive its most definitive statement and to constitute his lasting contribution to the literature and thought of his age.

Hazlitt's aesthetics are grounded in his empiricism. Whether discussing "familiar style," the plays of Shakespeare, or the paintings of Titian, he insists upon fidelity to the "stubborn" particulars of experience and to their exact impression on the mind. His highest tributes are regularly reserved for those artists who, by an unusually sympathetic disposition of mind, are able to respond most fully to the individual phenomena of nature and human character, and to reveal these phenomena through the "gusto" or total affective power of the artistic representation. In other words, art becomes for Hazlitt a prime instrument of human knowledge. By this criterion he praises Shakespeare's protean ability to become whatever he contemplated, and criticizes contemporary poets, Wordsworth and Byron most notably, for their self-centered "aversion to outward fact." Keats's celebrated judgments of Shakespeare's "negative capability" and Wordsworth's "egotistical sublime" were shaped by Hazlitt's response to these writers and his evaluation of poetry as the guide to experience.

Works of art can function in still higher ways. Under the impulse of passion created by the particular, the imagination of the artist will instinctively seek out associated and analogous thoughts and images and join them to the particular in the artistic representation. In this way, Hazlitt argues, the imagination acts to unify a diversity of experience and to stamp it with a pattern of human significance.

Hazlitt was fond of illustrating this creative, value-giving power of the imagination with references to the works of Shakespeare and Milton, but he demonstrates it himself in his familiar essays. In "The Letter-Bell" and "A Farewell to Essay-Writing," the ringing of a bell or the familiar objects in a natural scene set off a series of associated memories that reveal the continuity of Hazlitt's personality and beliefs over a period of forty years, and lead to an evaluation of the moral temper and progress of his society.

The essays in this collection include Hazlitt's central statements on psychology and art, examples of his biographical criticism, his journalistic reporting, and his personal essays. Common to all of them is the stylistic prowess that has made Hazlitt one of the acknowledged masters of the English essay. What Coleridge observed of Hazlitt's conversation as early as 1803 is richly revealed in the writings of his maturity: "He sends well-headed & well-feathered Thoughts straight forwards to the mark with a Twang of a Bow-string." From the forceful opening of "On Reason and Imagination" through the mellow conclusion of "A Farewell to Essay-Writing," his style transmits the voice of a man passionately involved with his experience and communicating that involvement through all the devices of language and sentence structure. Above all, his style indicates a man who was committed throughout his life to the "stubbornness" of fact and to those imaginative creations that give order and meaning to the complexity of human experience.

J. R. N.

principal dates in the life
of William Hazlitt

1778   Born April 10, at Maidstone, Kent, where his father is Unitarian minister; brother John (b. 1767), sister Margaret (b. 1770).

1779–83   In Ireland, where father is minister to congregation at Bandon, County Cork.

1783–87   In America, living in New York, Philadelphia, and near Boston, where father founds first Unitarian church.

1787   Hazlitt family returns to England and settles at Wem, Shropshire.

1793–95   Studies for the ministry at the Unitarian New College at Hackney, near London.

1796   Abandons ministerial studies and returns to Wem for a period of independent reading in philosophy, literature, and politics.

1798   January, meets Coleridge; in early summer, visits Coleridge at Nether Stowey, Somersetshire, and meets Wordsworth.

1799   Studies painting under his brother in London.

1800–02   Itinerant painter in various parts of England; October, 1802, visits Paris to study and copy paintings at the Louvre.

1803   March, returns from Paris; meets Charles Lamb; summer and fall, in Lake District, where he renews acquaintance with Coleridge and Wordsworth and paints their portraits; leaves under scandalous circumstances for alleged assaults on country women.

1804   Paints celebrated portrait of Lamb.

1805   Publishes *Essay on the Principles of Human Action*.

1806   Publishes *Free Thoughts on Public Affairs*.

1807   Publishes *An Abridgment of the Light of Nature Pursued, by Abraham Tucker; The Eloquence of the British Senate;* and *A Reply to the Essay on Population, by the Rev. T. R. Malthus*.

1808   May, marries Sarah Stoddart and moves to Winterslow, Wiltshire.

1809   Publishes *A New and Improved Grammar of the English Tongue*.

1811   September, son William born.

1812   January–April, delivers lectures on the history of English philosophy; fall, appointed parliamentary reporter for *Morning Chronicle*.

1813   Appointed drama critic for *Morning Chronicle*.

1814   Begins writing for *Champion* (as art and drama critic), *Edinburgh Review*, and Leigh Hunt's *Examiner*.

1815   Contributes "Round Table" essays and theatrical criticism to *Examiner*.

1816   Publishes *Memoirs of the Late Thomas Holcroft*.

1817   Publishes *Round Table* and *Characters of Shakespeare's Plays*; appointed drama critic of the *Times*.

1818   January–March, delivers "Lectures on the English Poets" (published in May); publishes a collection of his theatrical criticism, *View of the English Stage*; November, begins to deliver "Lectures on the English Comic Writers."

1819   January, "Lectures on the English Comic Writers" completed (published in April); publishes *A Letter to William Gifford, Esq.* and *Political Essays*; November–December, delivers "Lectures

on the Dramatic Literature of the Age of Elizabeth" (published in January, 1820); Hazlitt and
his wife no longer live together.

1820   Begins contributing dramatic criticism and "Table
Talks" to *London Magazine*; July, father dies;
August, meets Sarah Walker.

1821   Publishes *Table Talk or, Original Essays*.

1822   Begins contributing "Table Talks" to *New Monthly
Magazine*; January, departs for Scotland to arrange divorce (obtained in July); June, publishes
second volume of *Table Talk*; August, rejected by
Sarah Walker.

1823   January–July, contributes to Leigh Hunt's *Liberal*;
publishes *Characteristics: In the Manner of
Rochefoucault's Maxims* and *Liber Amoris*.

1824   Publishes *Sketches of the Principal Picture-Galleries
in England* and *Select British Poets or, New
Elegant Extracts from Chaucer to the Present
Time, with Critical Remarks*; marries Mrs. Isa-
bella Bridgewater; extended tour of continent
(August, 1824–October, 1825).

1825   Publishes *Spirit of the Age: or Contemporary Portraits*.

1826   Publishes *Plain Speaker* and *Notes of a Journey
through France and Italy*; July, 1826–October,
1827, in Paris, writing *Life of Napoleon*.

1827   Separated from his second wife.

1828   Publishes first two volumes of *Life of Napoleon*;
July–September(?), in Paris for further work on
Life of Napoleon; begins contributions to the
weekly *Atlas* (December, 1828–April, 1830).

1830   Publishes *Conversations of James Northcote, Esq.,
R.A.*, and final volumes of *Life of Napoleon*;
September 18, dies in London.

On Reason
and Imagination

I hate people who have no notion of any thing but generalities, and forms, and creeds, and naked propositions, even worse than I dislike those who cannot for the soul of them arrive at the comprehension of an abstract idea. There are those (even among philosophers) who, deeming that all truth is contained within certain outlines and common topics, if you proceed to add colour or relief from individuality, protest against the use of rhetoric as an illogical thing; and if you drop a hint of pleasure or pain as ever entering into "this breathing world,"[1] raise a prodigious outcry against all appeals to the passions.

It is, I confess, strange to me that men who pretend to more than usual accuracy in distinguishing and analysing, should insist that in treating of human nature, of moral good and evil, the nominal differences are alone of any value, or that in describing the feelings and motives of men, any thing that conveys the smallest idea of what those feelings are in any given circumstances, or can by parity of reason ever be in any others, is a deliberate attempt at artifice and delusion—as if a knowledge or representation of things as they really exist (rules and definitions apart) was a proportionable departure from the truth. They stick to the table of contents, and never open the volume of the mind. They are for having maps, not pictures of the world we live in: as much as to say that a

Note: At the end of each essay is indicated, to the left, the date of its original publication; and to the right, the date of its final publication during Hazlitt's lifetime. Where both dates appear, the text of the second date has been adopted, embodying whatever final revisions Hazlitt wished to make in his text.
[1] *Richard III*, I, i, 21

1

bird's-eye view of things contains the truth, the whole truth, and nothing but the truth. If you want to look for the situation of a particular spot, they turn to a pasteboard globe, on which they fix their wandering gaze; and because you cannot find the object of your search in their bald "abridgements," tell you there is no such place, or that it is not worth inquiring after. They had better confine their studies to the celestial sphere and the signs of the zodiac; for there they will meet with no petty details to boggle at, or contradict their vague conclusions. Such persons would make excellent theologians, but are very indifferent philosophers.—To pursue this geographical reasoning a little farther. They may say that the map of a county or shire, for instance, is too large, and conveys a disproportionate idea of its relation to the whole. And we say that their map of the globe is too small, and conveys no idea of it at all.

> —— "In the world's volume
> Our Britain shows as of it, but not in it;
> In a great pool a swan's nest:" [2]

but is it really so? What! the county is bigger than the map at any rate: the representation falls short of the reality, by a million degrees, and you would omit it altogether in order to arrive at a balance of power in the non-entities of the understanding, and call this keeping within the bounds of sense and reason; and whatever does not come within those self-made limits is to be set aside as frivolous or monstrous. But "there are more things between heaven and earth than were ever dreamt of in this philosophy." [3] They cannot get them all in, *of the size of life*, and therefore they reduce them on a graduated scale, till they think they can. So be it, for certain necessary and general purposes, and in compliance with the infirmity of human intellect: but at other times, let us enlarge our conceptions to the dimensions of the original objects; nor let it be pretended that we have outraged truth and nature, because we have encroached on your diminutive mechanical standard. There is no language, no description that can strictly

[2] *Cymbeline*, III, iv, 140–42   [3] Cf. *Hamlet*, I, v, 166–7

come up to the truth and force of reality: all we have to do is to guide our descriptions and conclusions by the reality. A certain proportion must be kept: we must not invert the rules of moral perspective. Logic should enrich and invigorate its decisions by the use of imagination; as rhetoric should be governed in its application, and guarded from abuse by the checks of the understanding. Neither, I apprehend, is sufficient alone. The mind can conceive only one or a few things in their integrity: if it proceeds to more, it must have recourse to artificial substitutes, and judge by comparison merely. In the former case, it may select the least worthy, and so distort the truth of things, by giving a hasty preference: in the latter, the danger is that it may refine and abstract so much as to attach no idea at all to them, corresponding with their practical value, or their influence on the minds of those concerned with them. Men act from individual impressions; and to know mankind, we should be acquainted with nature. Men act from passion; and we can only judge of passion by sympathy. Persons of the dry and husky class above spoken of, often seem to think even nature itself an interloper on their flimsy theories. They prefer the shadows in Plato's cave to the actual objects without it.[4] They consider men "as mice in an air-pump,"[5] fit only for their experiments; and do not consider the rest of the universe, or "all the mighty world of eye and ear,"[6] as worth any notice at all. This is making short, but not sure work. Truth does not lie *in vacuo*,[7] any more than in a well. We must improve our concrete experience of persons and things into the contemplation of general rules and principles; but without being grounded in individual facts and feelings, we shall end as we began, in ignorance.

It is mentioned in a short account of the Last Moments of Mr. Fox, that the conversation at the house of Lord Holland [8] (where he died) turning upon Mr. Burke's

---

[4] **shadows . . . it** Plato's *Republic*, Book VII   [5] Expression borrowed from Edmund Burke's *Letter to a Noble Lord* (1796) [6] Wordsworth's "Tintern Abbey," ll. 105–106   [7] "in a void" [8] **Charles James Fox** (1749–1806), one of the most distinguished statesmen and politicians of his time **Lord Holland** (1773–1840), Fox's nephew

style, that Noble Person objected to it as too gaudy and meretricious, and said that it was more profuse of flowers than fruit. On which Mr. Fox observed, that though this was a common objection, it appeared to him altogether an unfounded one; that on the contrary, the flowers often concealed the fruit beneath them, and the ornaments of style were rather an hindrance than an advantage to the sentiments they were meant to set off. In confirmation of this remark, he offered to take down the book, and translate a page any where into his own plain, natural style; and by his doing so, Lord Holland was convinced that he had often missed the thought from having his attention drawn off to the dazzling imagery. Thus people continually find fault with the colours of style as incompatible with the truth of the reasoning, but without any foundation whatever. If it were a question about the figure of two triangles, and any person were to object that one triangle was green and the other yellow, and bring this to bear upon the acuteness or obtuseness of the angles, it would be obvious to remark that the colour had nothing to do with the question. But in a dispute whether two objects are coloured alike, the discovery, that one is green and the other yellow, is fatal. So with respect to moral truth (as distinct from mathematical), whether a thing is good or evil, depends on the quantity of passion, of feeling, of pleasure and pain connected with it, and with which we must be made acquainted in order to come to a sound conclusion, and not on the inquiry, whether it is round or square. Passion, in short, is the essence, the chief ingredient in moral truth; and the warmth of passion is sure to kindle the light of imagination on the objects around it. The "words that glow" are almost inseparable from the "thoughts that burn." [9] Hence logical reason and practical truth are *disparates*. It is easy to raise an outcry against violent invectives, to talk loud against extravagance and enthusiasm, to pick a quarrel with every thing but the most calm, candid, and qualified statement of facts: but there are enormities to which no words can do adequate justice. Are we then, in order to form a com-

[9] "words . . . burn" cf. Gray's "The Progress of Poesy," l. 110

plete idea of them, to omit every circumstance of aggrava-
tion, or to suppress every feeling of impatience that arises
out of the details, lest we should be accused of giving
way to the influence of prejudice and passion? This would
be to falsify the impression altogether, to misconstrue
reason, and fly in the face of nature. Suppose, for instance, that in the discussions on the Slave-Trade, a description to the life was given of the horrors of the *Middle Passage* (as it was termed), that you saw the manner
in which thousands of wretches, year after year, were
stowed together in the hold of a slave-ship, without air,
without light, without food, without hope, so that what
they suffered in reality was brought home to you in
imagination, till you felt in sickness of heart as one of
them, could it be said that this was a prejudging of the
case, that your knowing the extent of the evil disquali-
fied you from pronouncing sentence upon it, and that your
disgust and abhorrence were the effects of a heated imagination? No. Those evils that inflame the imagination
and make the heart sick, ought not to leave the head
cool. This is the very test and measure of the degree of
the enormity, and it involuntarily staggers and appals the
mind. If it were a common iniquity, if it were slight and
partial, or necessary, it would not have this effect; but it
very properly carries away the feelings, and (if you will)
overpowers the judgment, because it is a mass of evil so
monstrous and unwarranted as not to be endured, even in
thought. A man on the rack does not suffer the less, because the extremity of anguish takes away his command
of feeling and attention to appearances. A pang inflicted
on humanity is not the less real, because it stirs up sympathy in the breast of humanity. Would you tame down
the glowing language of justifiable passion into that of
cold indifference, of self-complacent, sceptical reasoning,
and thus take out the sting of indignation from the mind
of the spectator? Not, surely, till you have removed the
nuisance by the levers that strong feeling alone can set
at work, and have thus taken away the pang of suffering
that caused it! Or say that the question were proposed to
you, whether, on some occasion, you should thrust your
hand into the flames, and were coolly told that you were
not at all to consider the pain and anguish it might give

you, nor suffer yourself to be led away by any such idle appeals to natural sensibility, but to refer the decision to some abstract, technical ground of propriety, would you not laugh in your adviser's face? Oh! no; where our own interests are concerned, or where we are sincere in our professions of regard, the pretended distinction between sound judgment and lively imagination is quickly done away with. But I would not wish a better or more philosophical standard of morality, than that we should think and feel towards others as we should, if it were our own case. If we look for a higher standard than this, we shall not find it; but shall lose the substance for the shadow! Again, suppose an extreme or individual instance is brought forward in any general question, as that of the cargo of sick slaves that were thrown overboard as so much *live lumber* by the captain of a Guinea vessel, in the year 1775, which was one of the things that first drew the attention of the public to this nefarious traffic,[10] or the practice of suspending contumacious negroes in cages to have their eyes pecked out, and to be devoured alive by birds of prey—Does this form no rule, because the mischief is solitary or excessive? The rule is absolute; for we feel that nothing of the kind could take place, or be tolerated for an instant, in any system that was not rotten at the core. If such things are ever done in any circumstances with impunity, we know what must be done every day under the same sanction. It shows that there is an utter deadness to every principle of justice or feeling of humanity; and where this is the case, we may take out our tables of abstraction, and set down what is to follow through every gradation of petty, galling vexation, and wanton, unrelenting cruelty. A state of things, where a single instance of the kind can possibly happen without exciting general consternation, ought not to exist for half an hour. The parent, hydra-headed injustice ought to be

---

[10] "See Memoirs of Granville Sharp, by Prince Hoare, Esq." (Hazlitt's note). Granville Sharp (1735–1813), English humanitarian and a leading opponent of the slave trade. His *Memoirs* were published in 1820. The atrocity to which Hazlitt refers, the drowning of 132 negro slaves, occurred in 1781; Sharp was largely responsible for bringing it to the attention of the public and encouraging legal proceedings against the perpetrators

crushed at once with all its viper brood. Practices, the mention of which makes the flesh creep, and that affront the light of day, ought to be put down the instant they are known, without inquiry and without repeal.

There was an example of eloquent moral reasoning connected with this subject, given in the work just referred to, which was not the less solid and profound, because it was produced by a burst of strong personal and momentary feeling. It is what follows:— "The name of a person having been mentioned in the presence of Naimbanna (a young African chieftain), who was understood by him to have publicly asserted something very degrading to the general character of Africans, he broke out into violent and vindictive language. He was immediately reminded of the Christian duty of forgiving his enemies; upon which he answered nearly in the following words:—'If a man should rob me of my money, I can forgive him; if a man should shoot at me, or try to stab me, I can forgive him; if a man should sell me and all my family to a slave-ship, so that we should pass all the rest of our days in slavery in the West Indies, I can forgive him; but' (added he, rising from his seat with much emotion) 'if a man takes away the character of the people of my country, I never can forgive him.' Being asked why he would not extend his forgiveness to those who took away the character of the people of his country, he answered: 'If a man should try to kill me, or should sell me and my family for slaves, he would do an injury to as many as he might kill or sell; but if any one takes away the character of Black people, that man injures Black people all over the world; and when he has once taken away their character, there is nothing which he may not do to Black people ever after. That man, for instance, will beat Black men, and say, *Oh, it is only a Black man, why should not I beat him?* That man will make slaves of Black people; for, when he has taken away their character, he will say, *Oh, they are only Black people, why should not I make them slaves?* That man will take away all the people of Africa if he can catch them; and if you ask him, But why do you take away all these people? he will say, *Oh! they are only Black people—they are not like White people—why should I not take them?* That is the reason why I cannot forgive the man who takes away the character of the people of my country.' "—MEMOIRS OF GRANVILLE SHARP, p. 369.

I conceive more real light and vital heat is thrown into the argument by this struggle of natural feeling to relieve itself from the weight of a false and injurious imputation, than would be added to it by twenty volumes of tables and calculations of the *pros* and *cons* of right and wrong, of utility and inutility, in Mr. Bentham's handwriting. In allusion to this celebrated person's theory of morals, I will here go a step farther, and deny that the dry calculation of consequences is the sole and unqualified test of right and wrong; for we are to take into the account (as well) the re-action of these consequences upon the mind of the individual and the community. In morals, the cultivation of a *moral sense* is not the last thing to be attended to—nay, it is the first. Almost the only unsophisticated or spirited remark that we meet with in Paley's Moral Philosophy, is one which is also to be found in Tucker's Light of Nature[11]—namely, that in dispensing charity to common beggars we are not to consider so much the good it may do the object of it, as the harm it will do the person who refuses it. A sense of compassion is involuntarily excited by the immediate appearance of distress, and a violence and injury is done to the kindly feelings by withholding the obvious relief, the trifling pittance in our power. This is a remark, I think, worthy of the ingenious and amiable author from whom Paley borrowed it. So with respect to the atrocities committed in the Slave-Trade, it could not be set up as a doubtful plea in their favour, that the actual and intolerable sufferings inflicted on the individuals were compensated by certain advantages in a commercial and political point of view—in a moral sense they *cannot* be compensated. They hurt the public mind: they harden and

[11] **William Paley** (1743–1805), author of *Principles of Moral and Political Philosophy* (1785), popular and influential moral textbook, in large part based on the work of previous theologians and writers; among them the philosopher **Abraham Tucker** (1705–74), whose *Light of Nature Pursued* was published in 1768–78. Hazlitt published an abridgment of Tucker in 1807

sear the natural feelings. The evil is monstrous and palpable; the pretended good is remote and contingent. In morals, as in philosophy, *De non apparentibus et non existentibus eaden est ratio*.[12] What does not touch the heart, or come home to the feelings, goes comparatively for little or nothing. A benefit that exists merely in possibility, and is judged of only by the forced dictates of the understanding, is not a set-off against an evil (say of equal magnitude in itself) that strikes upon the senses, that haunts the imagination, and lacerates the human heart. A spectacle of deliberate cruelty, that shocks every one that sees and hears of it, is not to be justified by any calculations of cold-blooded self-interest—is not to be permitted in any case. It is prejudged and self-condemned. Necessity has been therefore justly called "the tyrant's plea." [13] It is no better with the mere doctrine of utility, which is the sophist's plea. Thus, for example, an infinite number of lumps of sugar put into Mr. Bentham's artificial ethical scales would never weigh against the pounds of human flesh, or drops of human blood, that are sacrificed to produce them. The taste of the former on the palate is evanescent; but the others sit heavy on the soul. The one are an object to the imagination: the others only to the understanding. But man is an animal compounded both of imagination and understanding; and, in treating of what is good for man's nature, it is necessary to consider both. A calculation of the mere ultimate advantages, without regard to natural feelings and affections, may improve the external face and physical comforts of society, but will leave it heartless and worthless in itself. In a word, the sympathy of the individual with the consequences of his own act is to be attended to (no less than the consequences themselves) in every sound system of morality; and this must be determined by certain natural laws of the human mind, and not by rules of logic or arithmetic.

The aspect of a moral question is to be judged of very much like the face of a country, by the projecting points, by what is striking and memorable, by that which

[12] "There is the same rule concerning things which are not apparent and things which do not exist"   [13] *Paradise Lost*, IV, 393–94

leaves traces of itself behind, or "casts its shadow before." [14] Millions of acres do not make a picture; nor the calculation of all the consequences in the world a sentiment. We must have some outstanding object for the mind, as well as the eye, to dwell on and recur to—something marked and decisive to give a tone and texture to the moral feelings. Not only is the attention thus roused and kept alive; but what is most important as to the principles of action, the desire of good or hatred of evil is powerfully excited. But all individual facts and history come under the head of what these people call *Imagination*. All full, true, and particular accounts they consider as romantic, ridiculous, vague, inflammatory. As a case in point, one of this school of thinkers declares that he was qualified to write a better History of India from having never been there than if he had, as the last might lead to local distinctions or party-prejudices; that is to say, that he could describe a country better at second-hand than from original observation, or that from having seen no one object, place, or person, he could do ampler justice to the whole. It might be maintained, much on the same principle, that an artist would paint a better likeness of a person after he was dead, from description or different sketches of the face, than from having seen the individual living man. On the contrary, I humbly conceive that the seeing half a dozen wandering Lascars[15] in the streets of London gives one a better idea of the soul of India, that cradle of the world, and (as it were) garden of the sun, than all the charts, records, and statistical reports that can be sent over, even under the classical administration of Mr. Canning. *Ex uno omnes*.[16] One Hindoo differs more from a citizen of London than he does from all other Hindoos; and by seeing the two first, man to man, you know comparatively and essentially what they

[14] Cf. Thomas Campbell's poem "Lochiel's Warning" (1802), l. 56 [15] **Lascars** native Indian sailors or soldiers [16] **George Canning** (1770–1827), a leading politician of his time, was President of the Board of Control of the East India Company from 1816 to 1820, and British Foreign Secretary from 1822 to 1827 *Ex uno omnes* "all from one", *Aeneid*, II, 65–66

are, nation to nation. By a very few specimens you fix the great leading differences, which are nearly the same throughout. Any one thing is a better representative of its kind, than all the words and definitions in the world can be. The sum total is indeed different from the particulars; but it is not easy to guess at any general result, without some previous induction of particulars and appeal to experience.

"What can we reason, but from what we know?" [17]

Again, it is quite wrong, instead of the most striking illustrations of human nature, to single out the stalest and tritest, as if they were most authentic and infallible; not considering that from the extremes you may infer the means, but you cannot from the means infer the extremes in any case. It may be said that the extreme and individual cases may be retorted upon us:—I deny it, unless it be with truth. The imagination is an *associating* principle; and has an instinctive perception when a thing belongs to a system, or is only an exception to it. For instance, the excesses committed by the victorious besiegers of a town do not attach to the nation committing them, but to the nature of that sort of warfare, and are common to both sides. They may be struck off the score of national prejudices. The cruelties exercised upon slaves, on the other hand, grow out of the relation between master and slave; and the mind intuitively revolts at them as such. The cant about the horrors of the French Revolution is mere cant—every body knows it to be so: each party would have retaliated upon the other: it was a civil war, like that for a disputed succession: the general principle of the right or wrong of the change remained untouched. Neither would these horrors have taken place, except from Prussian manifestos,[18] and treachery within:

[17] Pope's *Essay on Man*, I, 18   [18] **Prussian manifestos** Hazlitt refers to the Declarations of July 25 and 27, 1792, signed by the Duke of Brunswick, the leader of the allied forces supporting Louis XVI. The threats to the revolutionists contained in the Declarations consolidated and intensified opposition to the King

there were none in the American, and have been none in the Spanish Revolution. The massacre of St. Bartholomew[19] arose out of the principles of that religion which exterminates with fire and sword, and keeps no faith with heretics.—If it be said that nick-names, party watchwords, bugbears, the cry of "No Popery," &c. are continually played off upon the imagination with the most mischievous effect, I answer that most of these bugbears and terms of vulgar abuse have arisen out of abstruse speculation or barbarous prejudice, and have seldom had their root in real facts or natural feelings. Besides, are not general topics, rules, exceptions, endlessly bandied to and fro, and balanced one against the other by the most learned disputants? Have not three-fourths of all the wars, schisms, heart-burnings in the world begun on mere points of controversy?—There are two classes whom I have found given to this kind of reasoning against the use of our senses and feelings in what concerns human nature, *viz.* knaves and fools. The last do it, because they think their own shallow dogmas settle all questions best without any farther appeal; and the first do it, because they know that the refinements of the head are more easily got rid of than the suggestions of the heart, and that a strong sense of injustice, excited by a particular case in all its aggravations, tells more against them than all the distinctions of the jurists. Facts, concrete existences, are stubborn things, and are not so soon tampered with or turned about to any point we please, as mere names and abstractions. Of these last it may be said,

"A breath can *mar* them, as a breath has made:" [20]

and they are liable to be puffed away by every wind of doctrine, or baffled by every plea of convenience. I wonder that Rousseau gave into this cant about the want of soundness in rhetorical and imaginative reasoning; and was so fond of this subject, as to make an abridgment of Plato's rhapsodies upon it, by which he was led to expel

[19] **Spanish Revolution** of 1820 against Ferdinand VII, who was restored to power in 1823 **St. Bartholomew's Day Massacre** the slaughter of French Protestants on August 24, 1572, by King Charles IX [20] Goldsmith's *The Deserted Village*, l. 54

poets from his commonwealth.[21] Thus two of the most flowery writers are those who have exacted the greatest severity of style from others. Rousseau was too ambitious of an exceedingly technical and scientific mode of reasoning, scarcely attainable in the mixed questions of human life, (as may be seen in his SOCIAL CONTRACT [22] —a work of great ability, but extreme formality of structure) and it is probable he was led into this error in seeking to overcome his too great warmth of natural temperament and a tendency to indulge merely the impulses of passion. Burke, who was a man of fine imagination, had the good sense (without any of this false modesty) to defend the moral uses of the imagination, and is himself one of the grossest instances of its abuse.

It is not merely the fashion among philosophers—the poets also have got into a way of scouting individuality as beneath the sublimity of their pretensions, and the universality of their genius. The philosophers have become mere logicians, and their rivals mere rhetoricians; for as these last must float on the surface, and are not allowed to be harsh and crabbed and recondite like the others, by leaving out the individual, they become commonplace. They cannot reason, and they must declaim. Modern tragedy, in particular, is no longer like a vessel making the voyage of life, and tossed about by the winds and waves of passion, but is converted into a handsomely-constructed steam-boat, that is moved by the sole expansive power of words. Lord Byron has launched several of these ventures lately[23] (if ventures they may be called) and may continue in the same strain as long as he pleases. We have not now a number of *dramatis personae* affected by particular incidents and speaking according to their feelings, or as the occasion suggests, but each mounting the rostrum, and delivering his opinion on fate, fortune, and

[21] **Rousseau . . . commonwealth** Hazlitt refers to Rousseau's essay "De l'Imitation Théâtrale" (1764), a summary of remarks in Plato's *Laws* and the tenth book of the *Republic*   [22] **SOCIAL CONTRACT** Rousseau's revolutionary political text, published in 1762   [23] **Lord Byron . . . lately** Between 1816 and 1822, Byron wrote eight poetic dramas, of which the most famous are the "metaphysical" *Manfred* (1817) and *Cain* (1821)

the entire consummation of things. The individual is not of sufficient importance to occupy his own thoughts or the thoughts of others. The poet fills his page with *grandes pensées*.[24] He covers the face of nature with the beauty of his sentiments and the brilliancy of his paradoxes. We have the subtleties of the head, instead of the workings of the heart, and possible justifications instead of the actual motives of conduct. This all seems to proceed on a false estimate of individual nature and the value of human life. We have been so used to count by millions of late, that we think the units that compose them nothing; and are so prone to trace remote principles, that we neglect the immediate results. As an instance of the opposite style of dramatic dialogue, in which the persons speak for themselves, and to one another, I will give, by way of illustration, a passage from an old tragedy, in which a brother has just caused his sister to be put to a violent death.

> "BOSOLA. Fix your eye here.
> FERDINAND. Constantly.
> BOSOLA. Do you not weep?
> Other sins only speak; murther shrieks out:
> The element of water moistens the earth;
> But blood flies upward, and bedews the heavens.
> FERDINAND. Cover her face: mine eyes dazzle;
> she died young.
> BOSOLA. I think not so: her infelicity
> Seem'd to have years too many.
> FERDINAND. She and I were twins:
> And should I die this instant, I had lived
> Her time to a minute."
> DUCHESS OF MALFY, Act IV. Scene 2.[25]

How fine is the constancy with which he first fixes his eye on the dead body, with a forced courage, and then, as his resolution wavers, how natural is his turning his face away, and the reflection that strikes him on her youth and beauty and untimely death, and the thought that

---

[24] "great thoughts," "elevated conceptions"   [25] Tragedy by John Webster, published in 1623

they were twins, and his measuring his life by hers up to the present period, as if all that was to come of it were nothing! Now, I would fain ask whether there is not in this contemplation of the interval that separates the beginning from the end of life, of a life too so varied from good to ill, and of the pitiable termination of which the person speaking has been the wilful and guilty cause, enough to "give the mind pause?" [26] Is not that revelation as it were of the whole extent of our being which is made by the flashes of passion and stroke of calamity, a subject sufficiently staggering to have place in legitimate tragedy? Are not the struggles of the will with untoward events and the adverse passions of others as interesting and instructive in the representation as reflections on the mutability of fortune or inevitableness of destiny, or on the passions of men in general? The tragic Muse does not merely utter muffled sounds: but we see the paleness on the cheek, and the life-blood gushing from the heart! The interest we take in our own lives, in our successes or disappointments, and the *home* feelings that arise out of these, when well described, are the clearest and truest mirror in which we can see the image of human nature. For in this sense each man is a microcosm. What he is, the rest are—whatever his joys and sorrows are composed of, theirs are the same—no more, no less.

"One touch of nature makes the whole world kin." [27]

But it must be the genuine touch of nature, not the outward flourishes and varnish of art. The spouting, oracular, didactic figure of the poet no more answers to the living man, than the lay-figure of the painter does. We may well say to such a one,

> "Thou hast no speculation in those eyes
> That thou dost glare with: thy bones are
> marrowless,
> Thy blood is cold!" [28]

[26] Cf. *Hamlet*, III, i, 68   [27] Shakespeare's *Troilus and Cressida*, III, iii, 175   [28] *Macbeth*, III, iv, 94–96

Man is (so to speak) an endless and infinitely varied repetition: and if we know what one man feels, we so far know what a thousand feel in the sanctuary of their being. Our feeling of general humanity is at once an aggregate of a thousand different truths, and it is also the same truth a thousand times told. As is our perception of this original truth, the root of our imagination, so will the force and richness of the general impression proceeding from it be. The boundary of our sympathy is a circle which enlarges itself according to its propulsion from the centre—the heart. If we are imbued with a deep sense of individual weal or woe, we shall be awe-struck at the idea of humanity in general. If we know little of it but its abstract and common properties, without their particular application, their force or degrees, we shall care just as little as we know either about the whole or the individuals. If we understand the texture and vital feeling, we then can fill up the outline, but we cannot supply the former from having the latter given. Moral and poetical truth is like expression in a picture—the one is not to be attained by smearing over a large canvas, nor the other by bestriding a vague topic. In such matters, the most pompous sciolists[29] are accordingly found to be the greatest contemners of human life. But I defy any great tragic writer to despise that nature which he understands, or that heart which he has probed, with all its rich bleeding materials of joy and sorrow. The subject may not be a source of much triumph to him, from its alternate light and shade, but it can never become one of supercilious indifference. He must feel a strong reflex interest in it, corresponding to that which he has depicted in the characters of others. Indeed, the object and end of playing, "both at the first and now, is to hold the mirror up to nature," [30] to enable us to feel for others as for ourselves, or to embody a distinct interest out of ourselves by the force of imagination and passion. This is summed up in the wish of the poet—

---

[29] **sciolists** persons of little understanding or experience who pretend to knowledge   [30] *Hamlet*, III, ii, 24–25

To feel what others are, and know myself a man.[31]

If it does not do this, it loses both its dignity and its proper use.

1826

[31] Gray's "Hymn to Adversity," l. 48

On Genius
and Common Sense

We hear it maintained by people of more gravity than understanding, that genius and taste are strictly reducible to rules, and that there is a rule for every thing. So far is it from being true that the finest breath of fancy is a definable thing, that the plainest common sense is only what Mr. Locke would have called a *mixed mode*,[1] subject to a particular sort of acquired and undefinable tact. It is asked, "If you do not know the rule by which a thing is done, how can you be sure of doing it a second time?" And the answer is, "If you do not know the muscles by the help of which you walk, how is it you do not fall down at every step you take?" In art, in taste, in life, in speech, you decide from feeling, and not from reason; that is, from the impression of a number of things on the mind, which impression is true and well-founded, though you may not be able to analyse or account for it in the several particulars. In a gesture you use, in a look you see, in a tone you hear, you judge of the expression, propriety, and meaning from habit, not from reason or rules; that is to say, from innumerable instances of like gestures, looks, and tones, in innumerable other circumstances, variously modified, which are too many and too refined to be all distinctly recollected, but which do not therefore operate the less powerfully upon the

[1] **John Locke** (1632–1704), popularly regarded as the founder of English empirical philosophy. In his influential *Essay Concerning Human Understanding* (1690), Locke had used the term **mixed mode** to describe such complex and abstract ideas as "beauty," "theft," "obligation," which are the result of the mind's ordering and combination of the impressions of different kinds of sensible qualities

mind and eye of taste. Shall we say that these impressions (the immediate stamp of nature) do not operate in a given manner till they are classified and reduced to rules, or is not the rule itself grounded upon the truth and certainty of that natural operation? How then can the distinction of the understanding as to the manner in which they operate be necessary to their producing their due and uniform effect upon the mind? If certain effects did not regularly arise out of certain causes in mind as well as matter, there could be no rule given for them: nature does not follow the rule, but suggests it. Reason is the interpreter and critic of nature and genius, not their lawgiver and judge. He must be a poor creature indeed whose practical convictions do not in almost all cases outrun his deliberate understanding, or who does not feel and know much more than he can give a reason for.— Hence the distinction between eloquence and wisdom, between ingenuity and common sense. A man may be dextrous and able in explaining the grounds of his opinions, and yet may be a mere sophist, because he only sees one half of a subject. Another may feel the whole weight of a question, nothing relating to it may be lost upon him, and yet he may be able to give no account of the manner in which it affects him, or to drag his reasons from their silent lurking-places. This last will be a wise man, though neither a logician nor rhetorician. Goldsmith was a fool to Dr. Johnson in argument; that is, in assigning the specific grounds of his opinions: Dr. Johnson was a fool to Goldsmith in the fine tact, the airy, intuitive faculty with which he skimmed the surface of things, and unconsciously formed his opinions. Common sense is the just result of the sum-total of such unconscious impressions in the ordinary occurrences of life, as they are treasured up in the memory, and called out by the occasion. Genius and taste depend much upon the same principle exercised on loftier ground and in more unusual combinations. . . .

I shall here try to go more at large into this subject, and to give such instances and illustrations of it as occur to me.

One of the persons who had rendered themselves obnoxious to Government, and been included in a charge for high treason in the year 1794, had retired soon after into Wales to write an epic poem and enjoy the luxuries of a rural life.[2] In his peregrinations through that beautiful scenery, he had arrived one fine morning at the inn at Llangollen, in the romantic valley of that name. He had ordered his breakfast, and was sitting at the window in all the dalliance of expectation, when a face passed of which he took no notice at the instant—but when his breakfast was brought in presently after, he found his appetite for it gone, the day had lost its freshness in his eye, he was uneasy and spiritless; and without any cause that he could discover, a total change had taken place in his feelings. While he was trying to account for this odd circumstance, the same face passed again—it was the face of Taylor the spy; and he was no longer at a loss to explain the difficulty. He had before caught only a transient glimpse, a passing side-view of the face; but though this was not sufficient to awaken a distinct idea in his memory, his feelings, quicker and surer, had taken the alarm; a string had been touched that gave a jar to his whole frame, and would not let him rest, though he could not at all tell what was the matter with him. To the flitting, shadowy, half-distinguished profile that had glided by his window was linked unconsciously and mysteriously, but inseparably, the impression of the trains that had been laid for him by this person;—in this brief moment, in this dim, illegible short-hand of the mind he had just escaped the speeches of the Attorney and Solicitor-General over again; the gaunt figure of Mr. Pitt[3] glared by him; the walls of a prison enclosed him; and he felt the hands of the executioner near him, without knowing it till the tremor and disorder of his nerves gave information to his reasoning faculties that all was not well

---

[2] **One of the persons . . . life** John Thelwall (1764–1834), political radical and vigorous opponent of the crown. He was arrested on a charge of sedition in May, 1794, but was acquitted in the famous "Hardy Trials" of October–November, 1794. In 1801, he published his epic poem "Edwin of Northumbria" in the collection *Poems chiefly written in Retirement*   [3] **William Pitt** (1759–1806), prime minister from 1783 to 1801. He was responsible for the arrest and imprisonment of Thelwall and other "seditionists" in the celebrated case of 1794

within. That is, the same state of mind was recalled by
one circumstance in the series of association that had
been produced by the whole set of circumstances at the
time, though the manner in which this was done was
not immediately perceptible. In other words, the feeling
of pleasure or pain, of good or evil, is revived, and acts
instantaneously upon the mind, before we have time to
recollect the precise objects which had originally given
birth to it.[4] The incident here mentioned was merely,
then, one case of what the learned understand by the
association of ideas: but all that is meant by feeling or
common sense is nothing but the different cases of the
association of ideas, more or less true to the impression of
the original circumstances, as reason begins with the
more formal developement of those circumstances, or
pretends to account for the different cases of the association of ideas. But it does not follow that the dumb and
silent pleading of the former (though sometimes, nay
often mistaken) is less true than that of its babbling interpreter, or that we are never to trust its dictates without
consulting the express authority of reason. Both are imperfect, both are useful in their way, and therefore both
are best together, to correct or to confirm one another.
It does not appear that in the singular instance above
mentioned, the sudden impression on the mind was super-

[4] "Sentiment has the same source as that here pointed out. Thus
the *Ranz des Vaches,* which has such an effect on the minds of
the Swiss peasantry, when its well-known sound is heard, does not
merely recal to them the idea of their country, but has associated
with it a thousand nameless ideas, numberless touches of private
affection, of early hope, romantic adventure, and national pride,
all which rush in (which mingled currents) to swell the tide of
fond remembrance, and make them languish or die for home.
What a fine instrument the human heart is! Who shall touch it?
Who shall fathom it? Who shall 'sound it from its lowest note to
the top of its compass?' Who shall put his hand among the strings,
and explain their wayward music? The heart alone, when touched
by sympathy, trembles and responds to their hidden meaning!"
(Hazlitt's note). *Ranz des Vaches*, "the air of the cows," a
melody played to call the cattle in Switzerland. Its ability to stir
the hearts of Swiss soldiers serving in foreign lands was proverbial
in Hazlitt's time   **"sound . . . compass"** *Hamlet*, III, ii, 383–
84

stition or fancy, though it might have been thought so, had it not been proved by the event to have a real physical and moral cause. Had not the same face returned again, the doubt would never have been properly cleared up, but would have remained a puzzle ever after, or perhaps have been soon forgot.—By the law of association, as laid down by physiologists, any impression in a series can recal any other impression in that series without going through the whole in order: so that the mind drops the intermediate links, and passes on rapidly and by stealth to the more striking effects of pleasure or pain which have naturally taken the strongest hold of it. By doing this habitually and skilfully with respect to the various impressions and circumstances with which our experience makes us acquainted, it forms a series of unpremeditated conclusions on almost all subjects that can be brought before it, as just as they are of ready application to human life; and common sense is the name of this body of unassuming but practical wisdom. Common sense, however, is an impartial, instinctive result of truth and nature, and will therefore bear the test and abide the scrutiny of the most severe and patient reasoning. It is indeed incomplete without it. By ingrafting reason on feeling, we "make assurance double sure." [5]

> " 'Tis the last key-stone that makes up the arch—
> Then stands it a triumphal mark! Then men
> Observe the strength, the height, the why and when
> It was erected: and still walking under,
> Meet some new matter to look up, and wonder." [6]

But reason, not employed to interpret nature, and improve and perfect common sense and experience, is, for the most part, a building without a foundation.—The criticism exercised by reason then on common sense may be as severe as it pleases, but it must be as patient as it is severe. Hasty, dogmatical, self-satisfied reason is worse than idle fancy, or bigotted prejudice. It is systematic, ostentatious in error, closes up the avenues of knowledge,

[5] *Macbeth*, IV, i, 83 [6] "Epistle to Edward Sacvile," ll. 136–42, in Ben Jonson's *Under-Wood* (1640)

and "shuts the gates of wisdom on mankind." [7] It is
not enough to show that there is no reason for a thing,
that we do not see the reason of it: if the common feeling, if the involuntary prejudice sets in strong in favour
of it, if, in spite of all we can do, there is a lurking suspicion on the side of our first impressions, we must try
again, and believe that truth is mightier than we. So,
in offering a definition of any subject, if we feel a mis-
giving that there is any fact or circumstance omitted,
but of which we have only a vague apprehension, like a
name we cannot recollect, we must ask for more time,
and not cut the matter short by an arrogant assumption
of the point in dispute. Common sense thus acts as a
check-weight on sophistry, and suspends our rash and
superficial judgments. On the other hand, if not only no
reason can be given for a thing, but every reason is clear
against it, and we can account from ignorance, from
authority, from interest, from different causes, for the prev-
alence of an opinion or sentiment, then we have a right
to conclude that we have mistaken a prejudice for an
instinct, or have confounded a false and partial impression with the fair and unavoidable inference from general
observation. Mr. Burke said that we ought not to reject
every prejudice, but should separate the husk of prejudice
from the truth it encloses, and so try to get at the kernel
within; and thus far he was right. But he was wrong in
insisting that we are to cherish our prejudices, "because they are prejudices:" for if they are all well-founded,
there is no occasion to inquire into their origin or use;
and he who sets out to philosophise upon them, or make
the separation Mr. Burke talks of in this spirit and with
this previous determination, will be very likely to mistake
a maggot or a rotten canker for the precious kernel of
truth, as was indeed the case with our political sophist.

There is nothing more distinct than common sense
and vulgar opinion. Common sense is only a judge of
things that fall under common observation, or immediately come home to the business and bosoms of men.
This is of the very essence of its principle, the basis of
its pretensions. It rests upon the simple process of feel-

[7] Cf. Gray's *Elegy Written in a Country Churchyard*, l. 68

ing, it anchors in experience. It is not, nor it cannot be, the test of abstract, speculative opinions. But half the opinions and prejudices of mankind, those which they hold in the most unqualified approbation and which have been instilled into them under the strongest sanctions, are of this latter kind, that is, opinions, not which they have ever thought, known, or felt one tittle about, but which they have taken up on trust from others, which have been palmed on their understandings by fraud or force, and which they continue to hold at the peril of life, limb, property, and character, with as little warrant from common sense in the first instance as appeal to reason in the last. The *ultima ratio regum*[8] proceeds upon a very different plea. Common sense is neither priestcraft nor state-policy. Yet "there's the rub that makes absurdity of so long life;" [9] and, at the same time, gives the sceptical philosophers the advantage over us. Till nature has fair play allowed it, and is not adulterated by political and polemical quacks (as it so often has been), it is impossible to appeal to it as a defence against the errors and extravagances of mere reason. If we talk of common sense, we are twitted with vulgar prejudice, and asked how we distinguish the one from the other: but common and received opinion is indeed "a compost heap" of crude notions, got together by the pride and passions of individuals, and reason is itself the thrall or manumitted slave of the same lordly and besotted masters, dragging its servile chain, or committing all sorts of Saturnalian[10] licences, the moment it feels itself freed from it.—If ten millions of Englishmen are furious in thinking themselves right in making war upon thirty millions of Frenchmen, and if the last are equally bent upon thinking the others always in the wrong, though it is a common and national prejudice, both opinions cannot be the dictate of good sense: but it may be the infatuated policy of one or both governments to keep their subjects always at variance. If a few centuries ago all Europe believed in the infallibility of the Pope, this was not an opinion derived from the proper exercise or

[8] "utmost concern of kings" [9] Cf. *Hamlet*, III, i, 65, 68–69
[10] **Saturnalian** riotous or dissolute

erroneous direction of the common sense of the people: common sense had nothing to do with it—they believed whatever their priests told them. England at present is divided into Whigs and Tories, Churchmen and Dissenters: both parties have numbers on their side; but common sense and party-spirit are two different things. Sects and heresies are upheld partly by sympathy, and partly by the love of contradiction: if there was nobody of a different way of thinking, they would fall to pieces of themselves. If a whole court say the same thing, this is no proof that they think it, but that the individual at the head of the court has said it: if a mob agree for a while in shouting the same watch-word, this is not to me an example of the *sensus communis*; they only repeat what they have heard repeated by others. If indeed a large proportion of the people are in want of food, of clothing, of shelter, if they are sick, miserable, scorned, oppressed, and if each feeling it in himself, they all say so with one voice and one heart, and lift up their hands to second their appeal, this I should say was but the dictate of common sense, the cry of nature. But to wave this part of the argument, which it is needless to push farther, I believe that the best way to instruct mankind is not by pointing out to them their mutual errors, but by teaching them to think rightly on indifferent matters, where they will listen with patience in order to be amused, and where they do not consider a definition or a syllogism as the greatest injury you can offer them.

There is no rule for expression. It is got at solely by *feeling*, that is, on the principle of the association of ideas, and by transferring what has been found to hold good in one case (with the necessary modifications) to others. A certain look has been remarked strongly indicative of a certain passion or trait of character, and we attach the same meaning to it or are affected in the same pleasurable or painful manner by it, where it exists in a less degree, though we can define neither the look itself nor the modification of it. Having got the general clue, the exact result may be left to the imagination to vary, to extenuate or aggravate it according to circumstances. In the admirable profile of Oliver Cromwell after ——, the drooping eye-lids, as if drawing a veil over the fixed, penetrating glance, the nostrils somewhat distended, and lips compressed so as hardly to let the breath escape him, denote the character of the man for high-reaching policy and deep designs as plainly as they can be written. How is it that we decipher this expression in the face? First, by feeling it: and how is it that we feel it? Not by pre-established rules, but by the instinct of analogy, by the principle of association, which is subtle and sure in proportion as it is variable and indefinite. A circumstance, apparently of no value, shall alter the whole interpretation to be put upon an expression or action; and it shall alter it thus powerfully because in proportion to its very insignificance it shews a strong general principle at work that extends in its ramifications to the smallest things. This in fact will make all the difference between minuteness and subtlety or refinement; for a small or trivial effect may in given circumstances imply the operation of a great power. Stillness may be the result of a blow too powerful to be resisted; silence may be imposed by feelings too agonising for utterance. The minute, the trifling and insipid, is that which is little in itself, in its causes and its consequences: the subtle and refined is that which is slight and evanescent at first sight, but which mounts up to a mighty sum in the end, which is an essential part of an important whole, which has consequences greater than itself, and where more is meant than meets the eye or ear. We complain sometimes of littleness in a Dutch picture, where there are a vast number of distinct parts and objects, each small in itself, and leading to nothing else. A sky of Claude's[11] cannot fall under this censure, where one imperceptible gradation is as it were the scale to another, where the broad arch of heaven is piled up of endlessly intermediate gold and azure tints, and where an infinite number of minute, scarce noticed particulars blend and melt into universal harmony. The subtlety in Shakespear, of which there is an immense deal every where scattered up and down, is always the instrument of passion, the vehicle of character. The action of a man pulling his hat over his forehead is indif-

[11] **Claude Lorrain** (1600–82), distinguished French landscape painter

ferent enough in itself, and, generally speaking, may mean any thing or nothing: but in the circumstances in which Macduff is placed, it is neither insignificant nor equivocal.

"What! man, ne'er pull your hat upon your brows," &c.

It admits but of one interpretation or inference, that which follows it:—

"Give sorrow words: the grief that does not speak,
 Whispers the o'er-fraught heart, and bids it break." [12]

The passage in the same play, in which Duncan and his attendants are introduced commenting on the beauty and situation of Macbeth's castle, though familiar in itself, has been often praised for the striking contrast it presents to the scenes which follow.[13]—The same look in different circumstances may convey a totally different expression. Thus the eye turned round to look at you without turning the head indicates generally slyness or suspicion: but if this is combined with large expanded eye-lids or fixed eye-brows, as we see it in Titian's pictures, it will denote calm contemplation or piercing sagacity, without any thing of meanness or fear of being observed. In other cases, it may imply merely indolent enticing voluptuousness, as in Lely's[14] portraits of women. The langour and weakness of the eye-lids gives the amorous turn to the expression. How should there be a rule for all this beforehand, seeing it depends on circumstances ever varying, and scarce discernible but by their effect on the mind? Rules are applicable to abstractions, but expression is concrete and individual. We know the meaning of certain looks, and we feel how they modify one another in conjunction. But we cannot have a separate rule to judge of all their combinations in different degrees and circumstances, without foreseeing all those combinations, which is impossible: or if we did foresee them, we should only be where we are, that is, we could only make the rule as we now judge without it, from imagination

---

[12] *Macbeth*, IV, iii, 208–10   [13] *Macbeth*, I, vi   [14] **Sir Peter Lely** (1618–80), famous Dutch-English portrait painter

and the feeling of the moment. The absurdity of reducing expression to a preconcerted system was perhaps never more evidently shewn than in a picture of the Judgment of Solomon by so great a man as N. Poussin,[15] which I once heard admired for the skill and discrimination of the artist in making all the women, who are ranged on one side, in the greatest alarm at the sentence of the judge, while all the men on the opposite side see through the design of it. Nature does not go to work or cast things in a regular mould in this sort of way. I once heard a person remark of another—"He has an eye like a vicious horse." This was a fair analogy. We all, I believe, have noticed the look of an horse's eye, just before he is going to bite or kick. But will any one, therefore, describe to me exactly what that look is? It was the same acute observer that said of a self-sufficient prating music-master—"He talks on all subjects *at sight*"—which expressed the man at once by an allusion to his profession. The coincidence was indeed perfect. Nothing else could compare to the easy assurance with which this gentleman would volunteer an explanation of things of which he was most ignorant; but the *nonchalance* with which a musician sits down to a harpsichord to play a piece he has never seen before. My physiognomical friend would not have hit on this mode of illustration without knowing the profession of the subject of his criticism; but having this hint given him, it instantly suggested itself to his "sure trailing." [16] The manner of the speaker was evident; and the association of the music-master sitting down to play at sight, lurking in his mind, was immediately called out by the strength of his impression of the character. The feeling of character, and the felicity of invention in explaining it, were nearly allied to each other. The first was so wrought up and running over, that the transition to the last was easy and unavoidable. When Mr. Kean was so much praised for the action of Richard in his last struggle with his triumphant antagonist, where he stands, after his sword is wrested from him, with his hands stretched out, "as if his will could not be disarmed,

---

[15] **Nicholas Poussin** (1595–1665), famous French painter of classical landscapes and historical subjects [16] Cf. *Hamlet*, II, ii, 47

and the very phantoms of his despair had a withering power," he said that he borrowed it from seeing the last efforts of Painter in his fight with Oliver.[17] This assuredly did not lessen the merit of it. Thus it ever is with the man of real genius. He has the feeling of truth already shrined in his own breast, and his eye is still bent on nature to see how she expresses herself. When we thorougly understand the subject, it is easy to translate from one language into another. Raphael, in muffling up the figure of Elymas the Sorcerer[18] in his garments, appears to have extended the idea of blindness even to his clothes. Was this design? Probably not; but merely the feeling of analogy thoughtlessly suggesting this device, which being so suggested was retained and carried on, because it flattered or fell in with the original feeling. The tide of passion, when strong, overflows and gradually insinuates itself into all nooks and corners of the mind. Invention (of the best kind) I therefore do not think so distinct a thing from feeling, as some are apt to imagine. The springs of pure feeling will rise and fill the moulds of fancy that are fit to receive it. There are some striking coincidences of colour in well-composed pictures, as in a straggling weed in the foreground streaked with blue or red to answer to a blue or red drapery, to the tone of the flesh or an opening in the sky:—not that this was intended, or done by rule (for then it would presently become affected and ridiculous), but the eye being imbued with a certain colour, repeats and varies it from

[17] **Edmund Kean** (1787–1833), a leading actor of the London stage. His performance of Richard III was considered unrivaled in his time "as if his will . . . power" Hazlitt quotes from his own review of Kean's first London performance of Richard III on February 12, 1814 **Edward Painter** (1784–1852) and **Tom Oliver** (1789–1864), boxers. Hazlitt refers to the match of May 17, 1814, in which Oliver bested Painter [18] **Raphael . . . Sorcerer** the subject of one of Raphael's famous cartoons, a series of colored drawings of scenes from the Acts of the Apostles to serve as models for tapestries for the Sistine Chapel at the Vatican. The cartoon to which Hazlitt refers depicts the appearance of Paul and Barnabas before the Roman governor of Cyprus to present the Christian faith. A magician, **Elymas**, attempts to thwart their success and is striken with blindness. Acts 13:6–12

a natural sense of harmony, a secret craving and appetite for beauty, which in the same manner soothes and gratifies the eye of taste, though the cause is not understood. *Tact, finesse,* is nothing but the being completely aware of the feeling belonging to certain situations, passions, &c. and the being consequently sensible to their slightest indications or movements in others. One of the most remarkable instances of this sort of faculty is the following story, told of Lord Shaftesbury, the grandfather of the author of the Characteristics.[19] He had been to dine with Lady Clarendon and her daughter, who was at that time privately married to the Duke of York (afterwards James II)[20] and as he returned home with another nobleman who had accompanied him, he suddenly turned to him, and said, "Depend upon it, the Duke has married Hyde's daughter." His companion could not comprehend what he meant; but on explaining himself, he said, "Her mother behaved to her with an attention and a marked respect that it is impossible to account for in any other way; and I am sure of it." His conjecture shortly afterwards proved to be the truth. This was carrying the prophetic spirit of common sense as far as it could go.—

1821   1824

[19] Anthony Ashley Cooper, **first Earl of Shaftesbury** (1621–83), controversial political leader. His grandson, **third Earl of Shaftesbury** (1671–1713), wrote *Characteristics of Men, Manners, Opinions, Times* (1711), an influential philosophic work
[20] **Lady Clarendon . . . James II** In September, 1660, the future king had secretly married Anne Hyde (1637–71), daughter of Edward Hyde, first Earl of Clarendon (1609–74), a leading statesman of his time and author of the famous *History of the Rebellion* (1702–04). The marriage was publicly acknowledged in December, 1660

The Same Subject
Continued

Genius or originality is, for the most part, *some strong quality in the mind, answering to and bringing out some new and striking quality in nature.*

Imagination is, more properly, the power of carrying on a given feeling into other situations, which must be done best according to the hold which the feeling itself has taken of the mind.[1] In new and unknown combinations, the impression must act by sympathy, and not by rule; but there can be no sympathy, where there is no passion, no original interest. The personal interest may in some cases oppress and circumscribe the imaginative faculty, as in the instance of Rousseau: but in general the strength and consistency of the imagination will be in proportion to the strength and depth of feeling; and it is rarely that a man even of lofty genius will be able to do more than carry on his own feelings and character, or some prominent and ruling passion, into fictitious and uncommon situations. Milton has by allusion embodied a great part of his political and personal history in the chief characters and incidents of Paradise Lost. He has, no doubt, wonderfully adapted and heightened them, but the elements are the same; you trace the bias and opinions of the man in the creations of the poet. Shakespear (almost alone) seems to have been a man of genius, raised above the definition of genius. "Born universal heir to all humanity," he was "as one, in suffering all who suffered nothing;"[2] with a perfect sympathy with

[1] "I do not here speak of the figurative or fanciful exercise of the imagination, which consists in finding out some striking object or image to illustrate another." (Hazlitt's note)   [2] *Hamlet*, III, ii, 71

31

all things, yet alike indifferent to all: who did not tamper with nature or warp her to his own purposes; who "knew all qualities with a learned spirit," [3] instead of judging of them by his own predilections; and was rather "a pipe for the Muse's finger to play what stop she pleased," [4] than anxious to set up any character or pretensions of his own. His genius consisted in the faculty of transforming himself at will into whatever he chose: his originality was the power of seeing every object from the exact point of view in which others would see it. He was the Proteus[5] of human intellect. Genius in ordinary is a more obstinate and less versatile thing. It is sufficiently exclusive and self-willed, quaint and peculiar. It does some one thing by virtue of doing nothing else: it excels in some one pursuit by being blind to all excellence but its own. It is just the reverse of the cameleon; for it does not borrow, but lend its colours to all about it: or like the glow-worm, discloses a little circle of gorgeous light in the twilight of obscurity, in the night of intellect, that surrounds it. So did Rembrandt. If ever there was a man of genius, he was one, in the proper sense of the term. He lived in and revealed to others a world of his own, and might be said to have invented a new view of nature. He did not discover things *out of* nature, in fiction or fairy land, or make a voyage to the moon "to descry new lands, rivers, or mountains in her spotty globe," [6] but saw things *in* nature that every one had missed before him, and gave others eyes to see them with. This is the test and triumph of originality, not to shew us what has never been, and what we may therefore very easily never have dreamt of, but to point out to us what is before our eyes and under our feet, though we have had no suspicion of its existence, for want of sufficient strength of intuition, or determined grasp of mind to seize and retain it. Rembrandt's conquests were not over the *ideal*, but the real. He did not contrive a new story or character, but we nearly owe to him a fifth part of painting,

---

[3] *Othello*, III, iii, 259   [4] Cf. *Hamlet*, III, ii, 75–76   [5] **Proteus** in Greek mythology, a seagod capable of assuming many shapes   [6] *Paradise Lost*, I, 290–91

the knowledge of *chiaroscuro*[7]—a distinct power and element in art and nature. He had a steadiness, a firm keeping of mind and eye, that first stood the shock of "fierce extremes" [8] in light and shade, or reconciled the greatest obscurity and the greatest brilliancy into perfect harmony; and he therefore was the first to hazard this appearance upon canvas, and give full effect to what he saw and delighted in. He was led to adopt this style of broad and startling contrast from its congeniality to his own feelings: his mind grappled with that which afforded the best exercise to its master-powers: he was bold in act, because he was urged on by a strong native impulse. Originality is then nothing but nature and feeling working in the mind. A man does not affect to be original: he is so, because he cannot help it, and often without knowing it. This extraordinary artist indeed might be said to have had a particular organ for colour. His eye seemed to come in contact with it as a feeling, to lay hold of it as a substance, rather than to contemplate it as a visual object. The texture of his landscapes is "of the earth, earthy" [9]—his clouds are humid, heavy, slow; his shadows are "darkness that may be felt," [10] a "palpable obscure;" [11] his lights are lumps of liquid splendour! There is something more in this than can be accounted for from design or accident: Rembrandt was not a man made up of two or three rules and directions for acquiring genius.

I am afraid I shall hardly write so satisfactory a character of Mr. Wordsworth, though he, too, like Rembrandt, has a faculty of making something out of nothing, that is, out of himself, by the medium through which he sees and with which he clothes the barrenest subject. Mr. Wordsworth is the last man to "look abroad into universality," [12] if that alone constituted genius: he looks at home into himself, and is "content with riches fineless." He would in the other case be "poor as winter," [13]

---

[7] *chiaroscuro* the treatment of light and dark in a painting [8] *Paradise Lost,* II, 599 [9] First Corinthians 15:47 [10] Exodus 10:21 [11] *Paradise Lost,* II, 406 [12] Francis Bacon's *Advancement of Learning* (1605), Book I [13] Cf. *Othello,* III, iii, 172–73

if he had nothing but general capacity to trust to. He is the greatest, that is, the most original poet of the present day, only because he is the greatest egotist. He is "self-involved, not dark." [14] He sits in the centre of his own being, and there "enjoys bright day." [15] He does not waste a thought on others. Whatever does not relate exclusively and wholly to himself, is foreign to his views. He contemplates a whole-length figure of himself, he looks along the unbroken lines of his personal identity. He thrusts aside all other objects, all other interests with scorn and impatience, that he may repose on his own being, that he may dig out the treasures of thought contained in it, that he may unfold the precious stores of a mind for ever brooding over itself. His genius is the effect of his individual character. He stamps that character, that deep individual interest, on whatever he meets. The object is nothing but as it furnishes food for internal meditation, for old associations. If there had been no other being in the universe, Mr. Wordsworth's poetry would have been just what it is. If there had been neither love nor friendship, neither ambition nor pleasure nor business in the world, the author of the Lyrical Ballads need not have been greatly changed from what he is— might still have "kept the noiseless tenour of his way," [16] retired in the sanctuary of his own heart, hallowing the Sabbath of his own thoughts. With the passions, the pursuits, and imaginations of other men, he does not profess to sympathise, but "finds tongues in the trees, books in the running brooks, sermons in stones, and good in every thing." [17] With a mind averse from outward objects, but ever intent upon its own workings, he hangs a weight of thought and feeling upon every trifling circumstance connected with his past history. The note of the cuckoo sounds in his ear like the voice of other years; the daisy spreads its leaves in the rays of boyish delight, that stream from his thoughtful eyes; the rainbow lifts its proud arch in heaven but to mark his prog-

---

[14] James Thomson's *The Castle of Indolence* (1748), stanza 57
[15] Milton's *Comus*, l. 382   [16] Gray's *Elegy Written in a Country Churchyard*, l. 76   [17] *As You Like It*, II, i, 16–17

ress from infancy to manhood; an old thorn is buried, bowed down under the mass of associations he has wound about it; and to him, as he himself beautifully says,

> ——"The meanest flow'r that blows can give
> Thoughts that do often lie too deep for tears." [18]

It is this power of habitual sentiment, or of transferring the interest of our conscious existence to whatever gently solicits attention, and is a link in the chain of association, without rousing our passions or hurting our pride, that is the striking feature in Mr. Wordsworth's mind and poetry. Others have felt and shown this power before, as Withers,[19] Burns, &c. but none have felt it so intensely and absolutely as to lend to it the voice of inspiration, as to make it the foundation of a new style and school in poetry. His strength, as it so often happens, arises from the excess of his weakness. But he has opened a new avenue to the human heart, has explored another secret haunt and nook of nature, "sacred to verse, and sure of everlasting fame." Compared with his lines, Lord Byron's stanzas are but exaggerated commonplace, and Walter Scott's poetry (not his prose) old wives' fables.[20] There is no one in whom I have been more disappointed than in the writer here spoken of, nor with whom I am more disposed on certain points to quarrel: but the love of truth and justice which obliges me to do this, will not suffer me to blench his merits. Do what he can, he cannot help being an original-minded man. His poetry is not servile. While the cuckoo returns in the spring, while the daisy looks bright in the sun, while the rainbow lifts its head above the storm—

[18] **The note of the cuckoo . . . tears** Hazlitt refers to various poems by Wordsworth: "To the Cuckoo" (1807); "My Heart Leaps up When I Behold" (1807); "The Thorn" (1798); "Ode: Intimations of Immortality from Recollections of Early Childhood" (1807), ll. 203–4   [19] **George Wither** (1588–1667), miscellaneous poet and pamphleteer   [20] "Mr. Wordsworth himself should not say this, and yet I am not sure he would not." (Hazlitt's note)

"Yet I'll remember thee, Glencairn,
And all that thou hast done for me!" [21]

Sir Joshua Reynolds, in endeavouring to show that there
is no such thing as proper originality, a spirit emanating
from the mind of the artist and shining through his works,
has traced Raphael through a number of figures which he
has borrowed from Masaccio and others.[22] This is a bad
calculation. If Raphael had only borrowed those figures
from others, would he, even in Sir Joshua's sense, have
been entitled to the praise of originality? Plagiarism, I
presume, in so far as it is plagiarism, is not originality.
Salvator[23] is considered by many as a great genius. He
was what they call an irregular genius. My notion of genius
is not exactly the same as theirs. It has also been made a
question whether there is not more genius in Rembrandt's
Three Trees[24] than in all Claude Lorraine's landscapes?
I do not know how that may be: but it was enough for
Claude to have been a perfect landscape-painter.

Capacity is not the same thing as genius. Capacity may
be described to relate to the quantity of knowledge, however acquired; genius to its quality and the mode of acquiring it. Capacity is a power over given ideas or combinations of ideas; genius is the power over those which
are not given, and for which no obvious or precise rule
can be laid down. Or capacity is power of any sort: genius
is power of a different sort from what has yet been shown.
A retentive memory, a clear understanding is capacity, but
it is not genius. The admirable Crichton[25] was a person

---

[21] Burns's "Lament for James, Earl of Glencairn," ll. 79–80
[22] **Sir Joshua Reynolds'** *Discourses* VI and XII **Masaccio To-
maso Guidi** (1401–c.1428), Florentine painter, whose frescoes
in the Church of the Carmine in Florence were influential on
Raphael, Michelangelo, and other painters of the time [23] **Salvator Rosa** (1615–1673), Neapolitan landscape painter of great
reputation in eighteenth-century England [24] *Three Trees* Rembrandt's most famous landscape, an etching of 1643 [25] **admirable Crichton** James Crichton (1560?–1582), a young Scotsman
who achieved a legendary reputation for his phenomenal memory,
wide learning, and great oratorical skills. "Admirable Crichton"
is a term applied to persons with prodigious and precocious talents

of prodigious capacity; but there is no proof (that I know) that he had an atom of genius. His verses that remain are dull and sterile. He could learn all that was known of any subject: he could do any thing if others could show him the way to do it. This was very wonderful: but that is all you can say of it. It requires a good capacity to play well at chess: but, after all, it is a game of skill, and not of genius. Know what you will of it, the understanding still moves in certain tracks in which others have trod before it, quicker or slower, with more or less comprehension and presence of mind. The greatest skill strikes out nothing for itself, from its own peculiar resources; the nature of the game is a thing determinate and fixed: there is no royal or poetical road to check-mate your adversary. There is no place for genius but in the indefinite and unknown. The discovery of the binomial theorem was an effort of genius; but there was none shown in Jedediah Buxton's[26] being able to multiply 9 figures by 9 in his head. If he could have multiplied 90 figures by 90 instead of 9, it would have been equally useless toil and trouble.[27] He is a man of capacity who possesses considerable intellectual riches: he is a man of genius who finds out a vein of new ore.

[26] **Jedediah Buxton** (1707–72), an illiterate Derbyshire farm-worker who possessed extraordinary arithmetical skills   [27] "The only good thing I ever heard come of this man's singular faculty of memory was the following. A gentleman was mentioning his having been sent up to London from the place where he lived to see Garrick act. When he went back into the country, he was asked what he thought of the player and the play. 'Oh!' he said, 'he did not know: he had only seen a little man strut about the stage, and repeat 7956 words.' We all laughed at this, but a person in one corner of the room, holding one hand to his forehead, and seeming mightily delighted, called out, 'Ay, indeed! And pray, was he found to be correct?' This was the supererogation of literal matter-of-fact curiosity. Jedediah Buxton's counting the number of words was idle enough; but here was a fellow who wanted some one to count them over again to see if he was correct.

'The force of *dulness* could not farther go!' "

(Hazlitt's note)   'The force . . . go' cf. Dryden's "Lines Printed Under the Engraved Portrait of Milton" (1688), l. 5

Originality is the seeing nature differently from others, and yet as it is in itself. It is not singularity or affectation, but the discovery of new and valuable truth. All the world do not see the whole meaning of any object they have been looking at. Habit blinds them to some things: short-sightedness to others. Every mind is not a gauge and meas-ure of truth. Nature has her surface and her dark recesses. She is deep, obscure, and infinite. It is only minds on whom she makes her fullest impressions that can penetrate her shrine or unveil her *Holy of Holies*. It is only those whom she has filled with her spirit that have the boldness or the power to reveal her mysteries to others. But nature has a thousand aspects, and one man can only draw out one of them. Whoever does this, is a man of genius. One displays her force, another her refinement, one her power of harmony, another her suddenness of contrast, one her beauty of form, another her splendour of colour. Each does that for which he is best fitted by his particular gen-ius, that is to say, by some quality of mind into which the quality of the object sinks deepest, where it finds the most cordial welcome, is perceived to its utmost extent, and where again it forces its way out from the fulness with which it has taken possession of the mind of the student. The imagination gives out what it has first absorbed by congeniality of temperament, what it has attracted and moulded into itself by elective affinity, as the loadstone draws and impregnates iron. A little originality is more esteemed and sought for than the greatest acquired talent, because it throws a new light upon things, and is peculiar to the individual. The other is common; and may be had for the asking, to any amount.

The value of any work is to be judged of by the quan-tity of originality contained in it. A very little of this will go a great way. If Goldsmith had never written any thing but the two or three first chapters of the Vicar of Wake-field, or the character of a Village-Schoolmaster,[28] they would have stamped him a man of genius. The Editors of Encyclopedias are not usually reckoned the first literary characters of the age. The works, of which they have the

[28] **Village-Schoolmaster** *The Deserted Village*, ll. 193–216

management, contain a great deal of knowledge, like chests or warehouses, but the goods are not their own. We should as soon think of admiring the shelves of a library; but the shelves of a library are useful and respectable. I was once applied to, in a delicate emergency, to write an article on a difficult subject for an Encyclopedia, and was advised to take time and give it a systematic and scientific form, to avail myself of all the knowledge that was to be obtained on the subject, and arrange it with clearness and method. I made answer that as to the first, I had taken time to do all that I ever pretended to do, as I had thought incessantly on different matters for twenty years of my life;[29] that I had no particular knowledge of the subject in question, and had no head for arrangement; and that the utmost I could do in such a case would be, when a systematic and scientific article was prepared, to write marginal notes upon it, to insert a remark or illustration of my own (not to be found in former Encyclopedias) or to suggest a better definition than had been offered in the text. There are two sorts of writing. The first is compilation; and consists in collecting and stating all that is already known of any question in the best possible manner, for the benefit of the uninformed reader. An author of this class is a very learned amanuensis of other people's thoughts. The second sort proceeds on an entirely different principle. Instead of bringing down the account of knowledge to the point at which it has already arrived, it professes to start from that point on the strength of the writer's individual reflections; and supposing the reader in possession of what is already known, supplies deficiencies, fills up certain blanks, and quits the beaten road in search of new tracts of observation or sources of feeling. It is in vain to object to this last style that it is disjointed, disproportioned, and irregular. It is merely a set of additions and corrections to other men's works, or to the common stock of human knowledge, printed separately. You might as well expect a continued chain of reasoning in the notes to a book. It skips all the trite, intermediate, level common-

---

[29] "Sir Joshua Reynolds being asked how long it had taken him to do a certain picture, made answer, 'All his life.'" (Hazlitt's note)

places of the subject, and only stops at the difficult passages of the human mind, or touches on some striking point that has been overlooked in previous editions. A view of a subject, to be connected and regular, cannot be all new. A writer will always be liable to be charged either with paradox or common-place, either with dulness or affectation. But we have no right to demand from any one more than he pretends to. There is indeed a medium in all things, but to unite opposite excellencies, is a task ordinarily too hard for mortality. He who succeeds in what he aims at, or who takes the lead in any one mode or path of excellence, may think himself very well off. It would not be fair to complain of the style of an Encyclopedia as dull, as wanting volatile salt; nor of the style of an Essay because it is too light and sparkling, because it is not a *caput mortuum.*[30] So it is rather an odd objection to a work that is made up entirely of "brilliant passages"—at least it is a fault that can be found with few works, and the book might be pardoned for its singularity. The censure might indeed seem like adroit flattery, if it were not passed on an author whom any objection is sufficient to render unpopular and ridiculous. I grant it is best to unite solidity with show, general information with particular ingenuity. This is the pattern of a perfect style: but I myself do not pretend to be a perfect writer. In fine, we do not banish light French wines from our tables, or refuse to taste sparkling Champagne when we can get it, because it has not the body of Old Port. Besides, I do not know that dulness is strength, or that an observation is slight, because it is striking. Mediocrity, insipidity, want of character is the great fault. *Mediocribus esse poetis non Dii, non homines, non concessêre columnae.*[31] Neither is this privilege allowed to prose-writers in our time, any more than to poets formerly.

It is not then acuteness of organs or extent of capacity that constitutes rare genius or produces the most exquisite

[30] **volatile salt** a light and lively character *caput mortuum,* "dead head," a heavy and lifeless character [31] "Neither Gods, nor men, nor booksellers have allowed poets to be mediocre." Horace's *Ars Poetica,* ll. 372–73

models of art, but an intense sympathy with some one beauty or distinguishing characteristic in nature. Irritability alone, or the interest taken in certain things, may supply the place of genius in weak and otherwise ordinary minds. As there are certain instruments fitted to perform certain kinds of labour, there are certain minds so framed as to produce certain *chef-d'oeuvres* in art and literature, which is surely the best use they can be put to. If a man had all sorts of instruments in his shop and wanted one, he would rather have that one than be supplied with a double set of all the others. If he had them all twice over, he could only do what he can do as it is, whereas without that one he perhaps cannot finish any one work he has in hand. So if a man can do one thing better than any body else, the value of this one thing is what he must stand or fall by, and his being able to do a hundred other things merely *as well* as any body else, would not alter the sentence or add to his respectability; on the contrary, his being able to do so many other things well would probably interfere with and incumber him in the execution of the only thing that others cannot do as well as he, and so far be a draw-back and a disadvantage. More people in fact fail from a multiplicity of talents and pretensions than from an absolute poverty of resources. I have given instances of this elsewhere. Perhaps Shakespear's tragedies would in some respects have been better, if he had never written comedies at all; and in that case, his comedies might well have been spared, though they might have cost us some regret. Racine, it is said, might have rivalled Moliere in comedy; but he gave up the cultivation of his comic talents to devote himself wholly to the tragic Muse. If, as the French tell us, he in consequence attained to the perfection of tragic composition, this was better than writing comedies as well as Moliere and tragedies as well as Crebillon.[32] Yet I count those persons fools who think it a pity Hogarth did not succeed better in serious subjects. The division of labour is an excellent principle in taste as well as in mechanics. Without this, I find from Adam

[32] **Prosper Jolyot de Crébillon** (1674–1762), a leading French tragedian of the eighteenth century

Smith, we could not have a pin made to the degree of perfection it is.[33] We do not, on any rational scheme of criticism, inquire into the variety of a man's excellences, or the number of his works, or his facility of production. Venice Preserved is sufficient for Otway's fame. I hate all those nonsensical stories about Lopez de Vega and his writing a play in a morning before breakfast.[34] He had time enough to do it after. If a man leaves behind him any work which is a model in its kind, we have no right to ask whether he could do any thing else, or how he did it, or how long he was about it. All that talent which is not necessary to the actual quantity of excellence existing in the world, loses its object, is so much waste talent or *talent to let*. I heard a sensible man say he should like to do some one thing better than all the rest of the world, and in every thing else to be like all the rest of the world. Why should a man do more than his part? The rest is vanity and vexation of spirit.[35] We look with jealous and grudging eyes at all those qualifications which are not essential; first, because they are superfluous, and next, because we suspect they will be prejudicial. Why does Mr. Kean play all those harlequin tricks of singing, dancing, fencing, &c.? They say, "It is for his benefit." [36] It is not for his reputation. Garrick indeed shone equally in comedy and tragedy. But he was first, not second-rate in both. There is not a greater impertinence than to ask, if a man is clever out of his profession. I have heard of peo-

[33] **Adam Smith** (1723–1790), moralist and political economist. Hazlitt refers to Smith's epoch-making treatise *The Wealth of Nations* (1776), Book I, chapter i [34] **Thomas Otway** (1652–85), leading dramatist of the Restoration period, author of classical and historical tragedies, of which *Venice Preserved* (1682) is the most famous **Lope Félix de Vega** (1562–1635), the father of Spanish drama, author of more than 500 plays [35] **vanity and vexation of spirit** Ecclesiastes 1:14 [36] **Mr. Kean . . . benefit** Hazlitt refers to the "benefit" (a theatrical presentation, the proceeds of which are given to the leading actor) of June 12, 1820, in which Kean followed his performance in *Venice Preserved* with a farce and a demonstration of his skill in singing, dancing, and impersonation

ple trying to cross-examine Mrs. Siddons.[37] I would as soon try to entrap one of the Elgin Marbles[38] into an argument. Good nature and common sense are required from all people: but one proud distinction is enough for any one individual to possess or to aspire to!

1821   1824

[37] **Sarah Siddons** (1755–1831), the most distinguished actress of her time   [38] **Elgin Marbles** famous collection of Greek sculpture brought to England by Lord Elgin (1766–1841) in 1806, and purchased for the nation by act of Parliament in 1816

On Gusto

Gusto in art is power or passion defining any object.—
It is not difficult to explain this term in what relates to
expression (of which it may be said to be the highest degree) as in what relates to things without expression, to
the natural appearances of objects, as mere colour or form.
In one sense, however, there is hardly any object entirely
devoid of expression, without some character of power
belonging to it, some precise association with pleasure or
pain: and it is in giving this truth of character from the
truth of feeling, whether in the highest or the lowest degree, but always in the highest degree of which the subject
is capable, that gusto consists.

There is a gusto in the colouring of Titian. Not only
do his heads seem to think—his bodies seem to feel. This
is what the Italians mean by the *morbidezza*[1] of his flesh-
colour. It seems sensitive and alive all over; not merely to
have the look and texture of flesh, but the feeling in itself.
For example, the limbs of his female figures have a luxurious softness and delicacy, which appears conscious of the
pleasure of the beholder. As the objects themselves in nature would produce an impression on the sense, distinct
from every other object, and having something divine in it,
which the heart owns and the imagination consecrates, the
objects in the picture preserve the same impression, absolute, unimpaired, stamped with all the truth of passion,
the pride of the eye, and the charm of beauty. Rubens
makes his flesh-colour like flowers; Albano's[2] is like ivory;
Titian's is like flesh, and like nothing else. It is as different

[1] *morbidezza*　a softness tender and attractive to the touch
[2] **Francesco Albano**　(1578–1660), Italian painter of religious and
mythological subjects

from that of other painters, as the skin is from a piece of
white or red drapery thrown over it. The blood circulates
here and there, and blue veins just appear, the rest is distinguished throughout only by that sort of tingling sensation to the eye, which the body feels within itself. This is
gusto.—Vandyke's flesh-colour, though it has great truth
and purity, wants gusto. It has not the internal character,
the living principle in it. It is a smooth surface, not a
warm, moving mass. It is painted without passion, with
indifference. The hand only has been concerned. The impression slides off from the eye, and does not, like the
tones of Titian's pencil, leave a sting behind it in the mind
of the spectator. The eye does not acquire a taste or appetite for what it sees. In a word, gusto in painting is where
the impression made on one sense excites by affinity those
of another.

Michael Angelo's forms are full of gusto. They every
where obtrude the sense of power upon the eye. His limbs
convey an idea of muscular strength, of moral grandeur,
and even of intellectual dignity: they are firm, commanding, broad, and massy, capable of executing with ease the
determined purposes of the will. His faces have no other
expression than his figures, conscious power and capacity.
They appear only to think what they shall do, and to know
that they can do it. This is what is meant by saying that
his style is hard and masculine. It is the reverse of Correggio's,[3] which is effeminate. That is, the gusto of Michael Angelo consists in expressing energy of will without
proportionable sensibility, Correggio's in expressing exquisite sensibility without energy of will. In Correggio's
faces as well as figures we see neither bones nor muscles,
but then what a soul is there, full of sweetness and of grace
—pure, playful, soft, angelical! There is sentiment enough
in a hand painted by Correggio to set up a school of history painters. Whenever we look at the hands of Correggio's women or of Raphael's, we always wish to touch
them.

Again, Titian's landscapes have a prodigious gusto,

[3] Antonio Allegri da Correggio (1494–1534), leading Italian
painter of his time

both in the colouring and forms. We shall never forget one that we saw many years ago in the Orleans Gallery of Acteon hunting.[4] It had a brown, mellow, autumnal look. The sky was of the colour of stone. The winds seemed to sing through the rustling branches of the trees, and already you might hear the twanging of bows resound through the tangled mazes of the wood. Mr. West,[5] we understand, has this landscape. He will know if this description of it is just. The landscape back-ground of the St Peter Martyr[6] is another well known instance of the power of this great painter to give a romantic interest and an appropriate character to the objects of his pencil, where every circumstance adds to the effect of the scene,—the bold trunks of the tall forest trees, the trailing ground plants, with that cold convent spire rising in the distance, amidst the blue sapphire mountains and the golden sky.

Rubens has a great deal of gusto in his Fauns and Satyrs, and in all that expresses motion, but in nothing else. Rembrandt has it in every thing; every thing in his pictures has a tangible character. If he puts a diamond in the ear of a Burgomaster's wife, it is of the first water; and his furs and stuffs are proof against a Russian winter. Raphael's gusto was only in expression; he had no idea of the character of any thing but the human form. The dryness and poverty of his style in other respects is a phenomenon in the art. His trees are like sprigs of grass stuck in a book of botanical specimens. Was it that R[...] never had time to go beyond the walls of Rome? Th[...]

[4] **Orleans Gallery** a celebrated exhibition of Italian paintings, from the collection of the Duc d'Orleans, shown in London in 1798–99. Hazlitt had attended the exhibition, which he regarded as the formative influence on his taste in painting thereafter **Acteon** in Greek mythology, the hunter Acteon was turned into a stag and destroyed by his own dogs for daring to observe Diana bathing　[5] **Benjamin West** (1738–1820), American-born historical painter, who became one of the leading painters in England after 1763 and president of the Royal Academy　[6] **St Peter Martyr** a famous altarpiece painted by Titian in 1528–30, depicting the murder of Peter, a thirteenth-century Dominican friar and preacher against the Manichean heretics

was always in the streets, at church, or in the bath? He was not one of the Society of Arcadians.[7]

Claude's landscapes, perfect as they are, want gusto. This is not easy to explain. They are perfect abstractions of the visible images of things; they speak the visible language of nature truly. They resemble a mirror or a microscope. To the eye only they are more perfect than any other landscapes that ever were or will be painted; they give more of nature, as cognizable by one sense alone; but they lay an equal stress on all visible impressions; they do not interpret one sense by another; they do not distinguish the character of different objects as we are taught, and can only be taught, to distinguish them by their effect on the different senses. That is, his eye wanted imagination: it did not strongly sympathize with his other faculties. He saw the atmosphere, but he did not feel it. He painted the trunk of a tree or a rock in the foreground as smooth— with as complete an abstraction of the gross, tangible impression, as any other part of the picture; his trees are perfectly beautiful, but quite immoveable; they have a look of enchantment. In short, his landscapes are unequalled imitations of nature, released from its subjection to the elements,—as if all objects were become a delightful fairy vision, and the eye had rarefied and refined away the other senses.

The gusto in the Greek statues is of a very singular kind. The sense of perfect form nearly occupies the whole mind, and hardly suffers it to dwell on any other feeling. It seems enough for them *to be*, without acting or suffering. Their forms are ideal, spiritual. Their beauty is power. By their beauty they are raised above the frailties of pain or passion; by their beauty they are deified.

[7] "Raphael not only could not paint a landscape; he could not paint people in a landscape. He could not have painted the heads or the figures, or even the dresses of the St Peter Martyr. His figures have always an *in-door* look, that is, a set, determined, voluntary, dramatic character, arising from their own passions, or a watchfulness of those of others, and want that wild uncertainty of expression, which is connected with the accidents of nature and the changes of the elements. He has nothing *romantic* about him." (Hazlitt's note)

The infinite quantity of dramatic invention in Shakspeare takes from his gusto. The power he delights to show is not intense, but discursive. He never insists on any thing as much as he might, except a quibble. Milton has great gusto. He repeats his blows twice; grapples with and exhausts his subject. His imagination has a double relish of its objects, an inveterate attachment to the things he describes, and to the words describing them.

> ——"Or where Chineses drive
> With sails and wind their *cany* waggons *light*."

* * * * * * * * * * * *

> "Wild above rule or art, *enormous* bliss." [8]

There is a gusto in Pope's compliments, in Dryden's satires, and Prior's tales;[9] and among prose-writers, Boccacio and Rabelais[10] had the most of it. We will only mention one other work which appears to us to be full of gusto, and that is the *Beggar's Opera*.[11] If it is not, we are altogether mistaken in our notions on this delicate subject.

May, 1816   1817

[8] *Paradise Lost*, III, 438–39; V, 297   [9] **Prior's tales** Hazlitt refers to "Idle Tales," a group of bawdy poems by Matthew Prior (1664–1721)   [10] **Giovanni Boccaccio** (1313?–75), author of the famous collection of bawdy tales *The Decameron* **François Rabelais** (1494–1553), author of the lusty satire *Gargantua and Pantagruel* (1532)   [11] *Beggar's Opera* John Gay's popular comic opera of London low-life, first presented in 1728

On Familiar Style

It is not easy to write a familiar style. Many people mistake a familiar for a vulgar style, and suppose that to write without affectation is to write at random. On the contrary, there is nothing that requires more precision, and, if I may so say, purity of expression, than the style I am speaking of. It utterly rejects not only all unmeaning pomp, but all low, cant phrases, and loose, unconnected, *slipshod* allusions. It is not to take the first word that offers, but the best word in common use; it is not to throw words together in any combinations we please, but to follow and avail ourselves of the true idiom of the language. To write a genuine familiar or truly English style, is to write as any one would speak in common conversation, who had a thorough command and choice of words, or who could discourse with ease, force, and perspicuity, setting aside all pedantic and oratorical flourishes. Or to give another illustration, to write naturally is the same thing in regard to common conversation, as to read naturally is in regard to common speech. It does not follow that it is an easy thing to give the true accent and inflection to the words you utter, because you do not attempt to rise above the level of ordinary life and colloquial speaking. You do not assume indeed the solemnity of the pulpit, or the tone of stage-declamation: neither are you at liberty to gabble on at a venture, without emphasis or discretion, or to resort to vulgar dialect or clownish pronunciation. You must steer a middle course. You are tied down to a given and appropriate articulation, which is determined by the habitual associations between sense and sound, and which you can only hit by entering into the author's meaning, as you must find the proper words and style to express yourself by fixing your thoughts on the subject you have to write about. Any one may mouth out a passage with a theatrical cadence, or get upon stilts to tell his thoughts: but to write or speak with propriety and simplicity is a more difficult task. Thus it is easy to affect a pompous style, to use a word twice as big as the thing you want to express: it is not so easy to pitch upon the very word that exactly fits it. Out of eight or ten words equally common, equally intelligible, with nearly equal pretensions, it is a matter of some nicety and discrimination to pick out the very one, the preferableness of which is scarcely perceptible, but decisive. The reason why I object to Dr. Johnson's style is, that there is no discrimination, no selection, no variety in it. He uses none but "tall, opaque words," taken from the "first row of the rubric:"—words with the greatest number of syllables, or Latin phrases with merely English terminations. If a fine style depended on this sort of arbitrary pretension, it would be fair to judge of an author's elegance by the measurement of his words, and the substitution of foreign circumlocutions (with no precise associations) for the mother-tongue.[1] How simple it is to be dignified without ease, to be pompous without meaning! Surely, it is but a mechanical rule for avoiding what is low to be always pedantic and affected. It is clear you cannot use a vulgar English word, if you never use a common English word at all. A fine tact is shewn in adhering to those which are perfectly common, and yet never falling into any expressions which are debased by disgusting circumstances, or which owe their signification and point to technical or professional allusions. A truly natural or familiar style can never be quaint or vulgar, for this reason, that it is of universal force and applicability, and that quaintness and vulgarity arise out of the immediate connection of certain words with coarse and disagreeable, or with confined ideas. The last form what we understand by *cant* or *slang* phrases.—To give an example of what is not very clear in the general statement. I should say that the phrase *To cut with a knife*, or *To cut a piece of wood*, is perfectly free from vulgarity, because it is perfectly com-

---

[1] "I have heard of such a thing as an author, who makes it a rule never to admit a monosyllable into his vapid verse. Yet the charm and sweetness of Marlow's lines depended often on their being made up almost entirely of monosyllables." (Hazlitt's note)

mon: but *to cut an acquaintance* is not quite unexception-
able, because it is not perfectly common or intelligible,
and has hardly yet escaped ɔut of the limits of slang
phraseology. I should hardly therefore use the word in this
sense without putting it in italics as a license of expression, to be received *cum grano salis*.[2] All provincial or bye-
phrases come under the same mark of reprobation—all
such as the writer transfers to the page from his fire-side or
a particular *coterie*, or that he invents for his own sole use
and convenience. I conceive that words are like money,
not the worse for being common, but that it is the stamp
of custom alone that gives them circulation or value. I
am fastidious in this respect, and would almost as soon
coin the currency of the realm as counterfeit the King's
English. I never invented or gave a new and unauthorised
meaning to any word but one single one (the term *impersonal* applied to feelings)[3] and that was in an abstruse
metaphysical discussion to express a very difficult distinction. I have been (I know) loudly accused of revelling in
vulgarisms and broken English. I cannot speak to that
point: but so far I plead guilty to the determined use of
acknowledged idioms and common elliptical expressions.
I am not sure that the critics in question know the one
from the other, that is, can distinguish any medium between formal pedantry and the most barbarous solecism.[4]
As an author, I endeavour to employ plain words and popular modes of construction, as were I a chapman[5] and
dealer, I should common weights and measures.

The proper force of words lies not in the words themselves, but in their application. A word may be a fine-
sounding word, of an unusual length, and very imposing
from its learning and novelty, and yet in the connection

---

[2] "with a grain of salt"　[3] (**the term *impersonal* applied to feelings**) Hazlitt refers to a passage in his first published work *An
Essay on the Principles of Human Action* (1805), in which he
argued that the love of self is not the wellspring of man's desires
and actions, but the consequence of his "disinterested love of good
as such. . . . In this sense self-love is in it's origin a perfectly
disinterested, or if I may so say *impersonal* feeling"　[4] **solecism**
mistake in the use of language　[5] **chapman** an itinerant merchant
or trader

in which it is introduced, may be quite pointless and ir-
relevant. It is not pomp or pretension, but the adaptation
of the expression to the idea that clenches a writer's meaning:—as it is not the size or glossiness of the materials,
but their being fitted each to its place, that gives strength
to the arch; or as the pegs and nails are as necessary to the
support of the building as the larger timbers, and more so
than the mere shewy, unsubstantial ornaments. I hate any
thing that occupies more space than it is worth. I hate to
see a load of bandboxes go along the street, and I hate
to see a parcel of big words without any thing in them.
A person who does not deliberately dispose of all his
thoughts alike in cumbrous draperies and flimsy disguises,
may strike out twenty varieties of familiar every-day language, each coming somewhat nearer to the feeling he
wants to convey, and at last not hit upon that particular
and only one, which may be said to be identical with the
exact impression in his mind. This would seem to shew
that Mr. Cobbett is hardly right in saying that the first
word that occurs is always the best.[6] It may be a very good
one; and yet a better may present itself on reflection or
from time to time. It should be suggested naturally, however, and spontaneously, from a fresh and lively conception of the subject. We seldom succeed by trying at improvement, or by merely substituting one word for another that we are not satisfied with, as we cannot recollect
the name of a place or person by merely plaguing ourselves
about it. We wander farther from the point by persisting
in a wrong scent; but it starts up accidentally in the memory when we least expected it, by touching some link in
the chain of previous association.

There are those who hoard up and make a cautious dis-
play of nothing but rich and rare phraseology;—ancient
medals, obscure coins, and Spanish pieces of eight. They
are very curious to inspect; but I myself would neither
offer nor take them in the course of exchange. A sprinkling
of archaisms is not amiss; but a tissue of obsolete expressions is more fit *for keep than wear*. I do not say I would

---

[6] **William Cobbett** (1762–1835), political controversialist, agri-
culturist, and writer. Hazlitt refers to his *Grammar of the English
Language* (1818), letter XXIII

not use any phrase that had been brought into fashion before the middle or the end of the last century; but I should be shy of using any that had not been employed by any approved author during the whole of that time. Words, like clothes, get old-fashioned, or mean and ridiculous, when they have been for some time laid aside. Mr. Lamb is the only imitator of old English style I can read with pleasure; and he is so thoroughly imbued with the spirit of his authors, that the idea of imitation is almost done away. There is an inward unction, a marrowy vein both in the thought and feeling, an intuition, deep and lively, of his subject, that carries off any quaintness or awkwardness arising from an antiquated style and dress. The matter is completely his own, though the manner is assumed. Perhaps his ideas are altogether so marked and individual, as to require their point and pungency to be neutralised by the affectation of a singular but traditional form of conveyance. Tricked out in the prevailing costume, they would probably seem more startling and out of the way. The old English authors, Burton, Fuller, Coryate, Sir Thomas Brown,[7] are a kind of mediators between us and the more eccentric and whimsical modern, reconciling us to his peculiarities. I do not however know how far this is the case or not, till he condescends to write like one of us. I must confess that what I like best of his papers under the signature of Elia (still I do not presume, amidst such excellence, to decide what is most excellent) is the account of *Mrs. Battle's Opinions on Whist*,[8] which is also the most free from obsolete allusions and turns of expression—

"A well of native English undefiled." [9]

[7] **Robert Burton** (1577–1640), author of *Anatomy of Melancholy* (1621) **Thomas Fuller** (1608–61), author of *Worthies of England* (1662) **Thomas Coryate** (1577?–1617), a famous traveller and author of *Coryats Crudities* (1611) **Sir Thomas Browne** (1605–82), author of *Religio Medici* (1643) [8] **Elia** the pseudonym adopted in 1820, under which Lamb wrote his most famous and characteristic essays **"Mrs. Battle's Opinions on Whist"** was first published in February, 1821 [9] *The Fairie Queene*, IV, ii, 32

To those acquainted with his admired prototypes, these
Essays of the ingenious and highly gifted author have
the same sort of charm and relish, that Erasmus's Col-
loquies[10] or a fine piece of modern Latin have to the
classical scholar. Certainly, I do not know any borrowed
pencil that has more power or felicity of execution than
the one of which I have here been speaking.

It is as easy to write a gaudy style without ideas, as it is
to spread a pallet of shewy colours, or to smear in a flaunt-
ing transparency.[11] "What do you read?"—"Words,
words, words."—"What is the matter?"—"*Nothing*," it
might be answered.[12] The florid style is the reverse of the
familiar. The last is employed as an unvarnished medium
to convey ideas; the first is resorted to as a spangled veil
to conceal the want of them. When there is nothing to be
set down but words, it costs little to have them fine. Look
through the dictionary, and cull out a *florilegium*, rival the
tulippomania.[13] *Rouge* high enough, and never mind the
natural complexion. The vulgar, who are not in the secret,
will admire the look of preternatural health and vigour;
and the fashionable, who regard only appearances, will be
delighted with the imposition. Keep to your sounding generalities, your tinkling phrases, and all will be well. Swell
out an unmeaning truism to a perfect tympany of style. A
thought, a distinction is the rock on which all this brittle
cargo of verbiage splits at once. Such writers have merely
verbal imaginations, that retain nothing but words. Or
their puny thoughts have dragon-wings, all green and gold.
They soar far above the vulgar failing of the *Sermo humi*

[10] **Desiderius Erasmus** (1466?–1536), the famous Renaissance
humanist, whose *Colloquia*, first published in 1519, were a series
of witty Latin dialogues or conversations on social and religious
questions, intended as a textbook for students of Latin style
[11] **transparency** a screen made of some translucent substance to
which figures, letters, or colors are applied, illuminated by means
of a light behind   [12] **"What do you read?"** . . . **answered** cf.
Hamlet, II, ii, 193–95   [13] **florilegium** literally, a collection of
flowers; by extension, an anthology or collection of fancy or flowery words   **tulippomania** a craze for tulips, originally applied to
seventeenth-century Dutchmen

obrepens[14]—their most ordinary speech is never short of an hyperbole, splendid, imposing, vague, incomprehensible, magniloquent, a cento[15] of sounding common-places. If some of us, whose "ambition is more lowly," pry a little too narrowly into nooks and corners to pick up a number of "unconsidered trifles," [16] they never once direct their eyes or lift their hands to seize on any but the most gorgeous, tarnished, thread-bare patch-work set of phrases, the left-off finery of poetic extravagance, transmitted down through successive generations of barren pretenders. If they criticise actors and actresses, a huddled phantasmagoria[17] of feathers, spangles, floods of light, and oceans of sound float before their morbid sense, which they paint in the style of Ancient Pistol.[18] Not a glimpse can you get of the merits or defects of the performers: they are hidden in a profusion of barbarous epithets and wilful rhodomontade.[19] Our hypercritics are not thinking of these little fantoccini[20] beings—

"That strut and fret their hour upon the stage"—[21]

but of tall phantoms of words, abstractions, *genera* and *species*, sweeping clauses, periods that unite the Poles, forced alliterations, astounding antitheses—

"And on their pens *Fustian* sits plumed." [22]

If they describe kings and queens, it is an Eastern pageant. The Coronation at either House is nothing to it. We get at four repeated images—a curtain, a throne, a sceptre, and a foot-stool. These are with them the wardrobe of a lofty imagination; and they turn their servile strains to

[14] "language crawling on the ground" cf. Horace's *Epistles*, II, i, 250–51   [15] **cento** verbal patchwork   [16] *Winter's Tale*, IV, iii, 26   [17] **phantasmagoria** a constantly shifting scene of differing and illusory shapes   [18] **Ancient Pistol** one of Falstaff's associates in *Merry Wives of Windsor*, *Henry IV*, and *Henry V*, and his standard-bearer ("Ancient"), whose speech is persistently overblown and rhetorical, even in the most mundane and sordid matters   [19] **rhodomontade** inflated language of boasting   [20] **fantoccini** puppets   [21] *Macbeth*, V, v, 25   [22] *Fustian* high-sounding but empty language   cf. *Paradise Lost*, IV, 988–9

servile uses. Do we read a description of pictures? It is not a reflection of tones and hues which "nature's own sweet and cunning hand laid on," [23] but piles of precious stones, rubies, pearls, emeralds, Golconda's mines,[24] and all the blazonry of art. Such persons are in fact besotted with words, and their brains are turned with the glittering, but empty and sterile phantoms of things. Personifications, capital letters, seas of sunbeams, visions of glory, shining inscriptions, the figures of a transparency, Britannia with her shield, or Hope leaning on an anchor, make up their stock in trade. They may be considered as *hieroglyphical* writers. Images stand out in their minds isolated and important merely in themselves, without any groundwork of feeling—there is no context in their imaginations. Words affect them in the same way, by the mere sound, that is, by their possible, not by their actual application to the subject in hand. They are fascinated by first appearances and have no sense of consequences. Nothing more is meant by them than meets the ear: they understand or feel nothing more than meets their eye. The web and texture of the universe, and of the heart of man, is a mystery to them: they have no faculty that strikes a chord in unison with it. They cannot get beyond the daubings of fancy, the varnish of sentiment. Objects are not linked to feelings, words to things, but images revolve in splendid mockery, words represent themselves in their strange rhapsodies. The categories of such a mind are pride and ignorance—pride in outside show, to which they sacrifice every thing, and ignorance of the true worth and hidden structure both of words and things. With a sovereign contempt for what is familiar and natural, they are the slaves of vulgar affectation—of a routine of high-flown phrases. Scorning to imitate realities, they are unable to invent any thing, to strike out one original idea. They are not copyists of nature, it is true: but they are the poorest of all plagiarists, the plagiarists of words. All is far-fetched, dear-bought, artificial, oriental in subject and allusion: all is mechanical, conventional, vapid, formal, pedantic in style and execution. They startle and confound the understand-

---

[23] *Twelfth Night*, I, v, 258   [24] **Golconda's mines** a source of diamonds in India; proverbial for great wealth

ing of the reader, by the remoteness and obscurity of their illustrations: they soothe the ear by the monotony of the same everlasting round of circuitous metaphors. They are the *mock-school* in poetry and prose. They flounder about between fustian in expression, and bathos in sentiment. They tantalise the fancy, but never reach the head nor touch the heart. Their Temple of Fame is like a shadowy structure raised by Dulness to Vanity,[25] or like Cowper's description of the Empress of Russia's palace of ice, as "worthless as in shew 'twas glittering"—

"It smiled, and it was cold!" [26]

1822   1824

[25] Hazlitt refers to two poems by Alexander Pope: *The Temple of Fame* (1715), a dream-vision (based on Chaucer), in which the poet is transported to the temple enshrining the heroes of human history and literature; and the *Dunciad* (1728–43), Pope's great satire on the intellectual mediocrity and corruption of his age, which involves the coronation of the poetaster Colley Cibber in the Temple of Dulness   [26] William Cowper's *The Task* (1785), V, 173–76

Jeremy Bentham [1]

Mr. Bentham is one of those persons who verify the old adage, that "A prophet has most honour out of his own country." [2] His reputation lies at the circumference; and the lights of his understanding are reflected, with increasing lustre, on the other side of the globe. His name is little known in England, better in Europe, best of all in the plains of Chili and the mines of Mexico. He has offered constitutions for the New World, and legislated for future times. The people of Westminster, where he lives, hardly dream of such a person; but the Siberian savage has received cold comfort from his lunar aspect, and may say to him with Caliban— "I know thee, and thy dog and thy bush!" [3] The tawny Indian may hold out the hand of fellowship to him across the GREAT PACIFIC. We believe that the Empress Catherine [4] corresponded with him; and we know that the Emperor Alexander [5] called upon him, and presented him with his miniature in a gold snuff-box, which the philosopher, to his eternal honour, returned. Mr. Hobhouse is a greater man at the hustings, Lord Rolle at Plymouth Dock; [6] but Mr. Bentham

[1] **Jeremy Bentham** (1748–1832), one of the leading social and political reformers of his age; exponent of the philosophy of Utilitarianism, which viewed man as a creature who desires to maximize his pleasures and avoid pains. According to Bentham, all social legislation and political activity, as well as all individual moral behavior, should conform to the "principles of utility," the securing of "the greatest happiness of the greatest number"
[2] Matthew 13:57 [3] Cf. *The Tempest*, II, ii, 144 [4] **Catherine the Great,** Empress of Russia from 1762 to 1796. Bentham had lived in Russia from 1785 to 1788 with the hope of realizing a number of his Utilitarian projects at the court of the "enlightened despot," who had embarked on an ambitious program of social and legal reform [5] **Alexander I,** Emperor of Russia from 1801 to 1825 [6] **Mr. Hobhouse . . . Plymouth Dock** John Cam Hobhouse (1786–1869), Byron's closest friend, member of Parliament from 1820 to 1833. **John Rolle** (1750–1842), member of Parliament for Devonshire from 1780 to 1796, subsequently a member of the House of Lords as Baron Rolle of Stevenstone. **Plymouth Dock** in Devonshire

would carry it hollow, on the score of popularity, at Paris or Pegu.[7] The reason is, that our author's influence is purely intellectual. He has devoted his life to the pursuit of abstract and general truths, and to those studies—

"That waft a *thought* from Indus to the Pole"—[8]

and has never mixed himself up with personal intrigues or party politics. He once, indeed, stuck up a hand-bill to say that he (Jeremy Bentham) being of sound mind, was of opinion that Sir Samuel Romilly[9] was the most proper person to represent Westminster; but this was the whim of the moment. Otherwise, his reasonings, if true at all, are true everywhere alike: his speculations concern humanity at large, and are not confined to the hundred or the bills of mortality.[10] It is in moral as in physical magnitude. The little is seen best near: the great appears in its proper dimensions, only from a more commanding point of view, and gains strength with time, and elevation from distance!

Mr. Bentham is very much among philosophers what La Fontaine[11] was among poets:—in general habits and in all but his professional pursuits, he is a mere child. He has lived for the last forty years in a house in Westminster, overlooking the Park, like an anchoret in his cell, reducing law to a system, and the mind of man to a ma-

[7] **Paris** between 1789 and 1793, Bentham addressed a number of publications on matters of political reform to the French National Assembly, and in 1792 was awarded honorary French citizenship **Pegu** name of a leading city and district in Burma, and the scene of considerable English and French military involvement in the late eighteenth and early nineteenth centuries. Hazlitt may be referring to Bentham's support for the emancipation of colonial territories   [8] Cf. Pope's *Eloisa to Abelard*, l. 58   [9] **Sir Samuel Romilly** (1757–1818), a leading spokesman for the reform of English criminal law, member of Parliament from 1806 to 1818   [10] that is, restricted to his immediate vicinity **the hundred** "a sub-division of a county or shire, having its own court" (*Oxford English Dictionary*) **bills of mortality** originally a published list of deaths and births in and around London, by extension, the area itself   [11] **Jean de La Fontaine** (1621–95), leading French writer and author of a famous collection of fables

chine. He scarcely ever goes out, and sees very little company. The favoured few, who have the privilege of the *entrée*, are always admitted one by one. He does not like to have witnesses to his conversation. He talks a great deal, and listens to nothing but facts. When any one calls upon him, he invites them to take a turn round his garden with him (Mr. Bentham is an economist of his time, and sets apart this portion of it to air and exercise)—and there you may see the lively old man, his mind still buoyant with thought and with the prospect of futurity, in eager conversation with some Opposition Member, some expatriated Patriot, or Transatlantic Adventurer, urging the extinction of Close Boroughs,[12] or planning a code of laws for some "lone island in the watery waste," [13] his walk almost amounting to a run, his tongue keeping pace with it in shrill, cluttering accents, negligent of his person, his dress, and his manner, intent only on his grand theme of UTILITY—or pausing, perhaps, for want of breath and with lack-lustre eye to point out to the stranger a stone in the wall at the end of his garden (overarched by two beautiful cotton-trees) *Inscribed to the Prince of Poets*, which marks the house where Milton formerly lived. To show how little the refinements of taste or fancy enter into our author's system, he proposed at one time to cut down these beautiful trees, to convert the garden where he had breathed the air of Truth and Heaven for near half a century into a paltry *Chrestomathic School*,[14] and to make Milton's house (the cradle of Paradise Lost) a thoroughfare, like a three-stalled stable, for the idle rabble of Westminster to pass backwards and forwards to it with their cloven hoofs. Let us not, however, be getting on too fast— Milton himself taught school! There is something not altogether dissimilar between Mr. Bentham's appearance,

[12] **Close Boroughs**   parliamentary districts completely in the purchase or control of one person, not open to contest or competition   [13] Cf. Pope's *Essay on Man*, I, 106   [14] *Chrestomathic* a Greek coinage meaning "conducive to useful learning." Hazlitt refers to Bentham's plan in 1815 to set up a model school "for the use of the middling and higher ranks in life," with a curriculum emphasizing the natural and physical sciences rather than the traditional study of the classics and theology

and the portraits of Milton, the same silvery tone, a few dishevelled hairs, a peevish, yet puritanical expression, an irritable temperament corrected by habit and discipline. Or in modern times, he is something between Franklin and Charles Fox, with the comfortable double-chin and sleek thriving look of the one, and the quivering lip, the restless eye, and animated acuteness of the other. His eye is quick and lively; but it glances not from object to object, but from thought to thought. He is evidently a man occupied with some train of fine and inward association. He regards the people about him no more than the flies of a summer. He meditates the coming age. He hears and sees only what suits his purpose, or some "foregone conclusion;" [15] and looks out for facts and passing occurrences in order to put them into his logical machinery and grind them into the dust and powder of some subtle theory, as the miller looks out for grist to his mill! Add to this physiognomical sketch the minor points of costume, the open shirt-collar, the single-breasted coat, the old-fashioned half-boots and ribbed stockings; and you will find in Mr. Bentham's general appearance a singular mixture of boyish simplicity and of the venerableness of age. In a word, our celebrated jurist presents a striking illustration of the difference between the *philosophical* and the *regal* look; that is, between the merely abstracted and the merely personal. There is a lack-adaisical *bonhommie* about his whole aspect, none of the fierceness of pride or power; an unconscious neglect of his own person, instead of a stately assumption of superiority; a good-humoured, placid intelligence, instead of a lynx-eyed watchfulness, as if it wished to make others its prey, or was afraid they might turn and rend him; he is a beneficent spirit, prying into the universe, not lording it over it; a thoughtful spectator of the scenes of life, or ruminator on the fate of mankind, not a painted pageant, a stupid idol set up on its pedestal of pride for men to fall down and worship with idiot fear and wonder at the thing themselves have made, and which, without that fear and wonder, would in itself be nothing!

Mr. Bentham, perhaps, over-rates the importance of his

[15] *Othello*, III, iii, 428

own theories. He has been heard to say (without any appearance of pride or affectation) that "he should like to live the remaining years of his life, a year at a time at the end of the next six or eight centuries, to see the effect which his writings would by that time have had upon the world." Alas! his name will hardly live so long! Nor do we think, in point of fact, that Mr. Bentham has given any new or decided impulse to the human mind. He cannot be looked upon in the light of a discoverer in legislation or morals. He has not struck out any great leading principle or parent-truth, from which a number of others might be deduced; nor has he enriched the common and established stock of intelligence with original observations, like pearls thrown into wine. One truth discovered is immortal, and entitles its author to be so: for, like a new substance in nature, it cannot be destroyed. But Mr. Bentham's *forte* is arrangement; and the form of truth, though not its essence, varies with time and circumstance. He has methodised, collated, and condensed all the materials prepared to his hand on the subjects of which he treats, in a masterly and scientific manner; but we should find a difficulty in adducing from his different works (however elaborate or closely reasoned) any new element of thought, or even a new fact or illustration. His writings are, therefore, chiefly valuable as *books of reference,* as bringing down the account of intellectual inquiry to the present period, and disposing the results in a compendious, connected, and tangible shape; but books of reference are chiefly serviceable for facilitating the acquisition of knowledge, and are constantly liable to be superseded and to grow out of fashion with its progress, as the scaffolding is thrown down as soon as the building is completed. Mr. Bentham is not the first writer (by a great many) who has assumed the principle of UTILITY as the foundation of just laws, and of all moral and political reasoning:—his merit is, that he has applied this principle more closely and literally; that he has brought all the objections and arguments, more distinctly labelled and ticketted, under this one head, and made a more constant and explicit reference to it at every step of his progress, than any other writer. Perhaps the weak side of his conclusions also is, that he has carried this single view of his subject too far, and not made sufficient allowance for the varieties of human nature, and the caprices and irregularities of the human will. "He has not allowed for the *wind*." [16] It is not that you can be said to see his favourite doctrine of Utility glittering everywhere through his system, like a vein of rich, shining ore (that is not the nature of the material)—but it might be plausibly objected that he had struck the whole mass of fancy, prejudice, passion, sense, whim, with his petrific, leaden mace, that he had "bound volatile Hermes," [17] and reduced the theory and practice of human life to a *caput mortuum* of reason, and dull, plodding, technical calculation. The gentleman is himself a capital logician; and he has been led by this circumstance to consider man as a logical animal. We fear this view of the matter will hardly hold water. If we attend to the *moral* man, the constitution of his mind will scarcely be found to be built up of pure reason and a regard to consequences: if we consider the *criminal* man (with whom the legislator has chiefly to do) it will be found to be still less so.

Every pleasure, says Mr. Bentham, is equally a good, and is to be taken into the account as such in a moral estimate, whether it be the pleasure of sense or of conscience, whether it arise from the exercise of virtue or the perpetration of crime. We are afraid the human mind does not readily come into this doctrine, this *ultima ratio philosophorum*,[18] interpreted according to the letter. Our moral sentiments are made up of sympathies and antipathies, of sense and imagination, of understanding and prejudice. The soul, by reason of its weakness, is an aggregating and exclusive principle; it clings obstinately to some things, and violently rejects others. And it must do so, in a great measure, or it would act contrary to its own nature. It needs helps and stages in its progress, and "all appliances and means to boot," [19] which can raise it to a partial conformity to truth and good (the utmost it is capable of) and bring it into a tolerable harmony with the universe. By aiming at too much, by dismissing collateral aids, by extending itself to the farthest verge of the

[16] Scott's *Ivanhoe*, chapter XIII   [17] *Paradise Lost*, III, 602–3
[18] "utmost concern of philosophers"   [19] *Henry IV, Part II*, III, i, 29

conceivable and possible, it loses its elasticity and vigour, its impulse and its direction. The moralist can no more do without the intermediate use of rules and principles, without the 'vantage ground of habit, without the levers of the understanding, than the mechanist can discard the use of wheels and pulleys, and perform every thing by simple motion. If the mind of man were competent to comprehend the whole of truth and good, and act upon it at once, and independently of all other considerations, Mr. Bentham's plan would be a feasible one, and *the truth, the whole truth, and nothing but the truth,* would be the best possible ground to place morality upon. But it is not so. In ascertaining the rules of moral conduct, we must have regard not merely to the nature of the object, but to the capacity of the agent, and to his fitness for apprehending or attaining it. Pleasure is that which is so in itself: good is that which approves itself as such on reflection, or the idea of which is a source of satisfaction. All pleasure is not, therefore (morally speaking) equally a good; for all pleasure does not equally bear reflecting on. There are some tastes that are sweet in the mouth and bitter in the belly; and there is a similar contradiction and anomaly in the mind and heart of man. Again, what would become of the *Posthaec meminisse juvabit*[20] of the poet, if a principle of fluctuation and reaction is not inherent in the very constitution of our nature, or if all moral truth is a mere literal truism? We are not, then, so much to inquire what certain things are abstractedly or in themselves, as how they affect the mind, and to approve or condemn them accordingly. The same object seen near strikes us more powerfully than at a distance: things thrown into masses give a greater blow to the imagination than when scattered and divided into their component parts. A number of mole-hills do not make a mountain, though a mountain is actually made up of atoms: so moral truth must present itself under a certain aspect and from a certain point of view, in order to produce its full and proper effect upon the mind. The laws of the affections are as necessary as those of optics. A calculation

[20] "It will delight us someday to have remembered these things" *Aeneid*, I, 203

of consequences is no more equivalent to a sentiment, than a *seriatim* enumeration of square yards or feet touches the fancy like the sight of the Alps or Andes.

To give an instance or two of what we mean. Those who on pure cosmopolite principles, or on the ground of abstract humanity, affect an extraordinary regard for the Turks and Tartars, have been accused of neglecting their duties to their friends and next-door neighbours. Well, then, what is the state of the question here? One human being is, no doubt, as much worth in himself, independently of the circumstances of time or place, as another; but he is not of so much value to us and our affections. Could our imagination take wing (with our speculative faculties) to the other side of the globe or to the ends of the universe, could our eyes behold whatever our reason teaches us to be possible, could our hands reach as far as our thoughts and wishes, we might then busy ourselves to advantage with the Hottentots, or hold intimate converse with the inhabitants of the Moon; but being as we are, our feelings evaporate in so large a space—we must draw the circle of our affections and duties somewhat closer—the heart hovers and fixes nearer home. It is true, the bands of private, or of local and natural affection, are often, nay in general, too tightly strained, so as frequently to do harm instead of good: but the present question is whether we can, with safety and effect, be wholly emancipated from them? Whether we should shake them off at pleasure and without mercy, as the only bar to the triumph of truth and justice? Or whether benevolence, constructed upon a logical scale, would not be merely *nominal*, whether duty, raised to too lofty a pitch of refinement, might not sink into callous indifference or hollow selfishness? Again, is it not to exact too high a strain from humanity, to ask us to qualify the degree of abhorrence we feel against a murderer by taking into our cool consideration the pleasure he may have in committing the deed, and in the prospect of gratifying his avarice or his revenge? We are hardly so formed as to sympathise at the same moment with the assassin and his victim. The degree of pleasure the former may feel, instead of extenuating, aggravates his guilt, and shows the depth of his malignity. Now the mind revolts against this by mere natural antipathy, if it is itself well-disposed; or the slow process of reason would afford but a feeble resistance to violence and wrong. The will, which is necessary to give consistency and promptness to our good intentions, cannot extend so much candour and courtesy to the antagonist principle of evil: virtue, to be sincere and practical, cannot be divested entirely of the blindness and impetuosity of passion! It has been made a plea (half jest, half earnest) for the horrors of war, that they promote trade and manufactures. It has been said, as a set-off for the atrocities practised upon the negro slaves in the West Indies, that without their blood and sweat, so many millions of people could not have sugar to sweeten their tea. Fires and murders have been argued to be beneficial, as they serve to fill the newspapers, and for a subject to talk of —this is a sort of sophistry that it might be difficult to disprove on the bare scheme of contingent utility; but on the ground that we have stated, it must pass for mere irony. What the proportion between the good and the evil will really be found in any of the supposed cases, may be a question to the understanding; but to the imagination and the heart, that is, to the natural feelings of mankind, it admits of none!

Mr. Bentham, in adjusting the provisions of a penal code, lays too little stress on the co-operation of the natural prejudices of mankind, and the habitual feelings of that class of persons for whom they are more particularly designed. Legislators (we mean writers on legislation) are philosophers, and governed by their reason: criminals, for whose controul laws are made, are a set of desperadoes, governed only by their passions. What wonder that so little progress has been made towards a mutual understanding between the two parties! They are quite a different species, and speak a different language, and are sadly at a loss for a common interpreter between them. Perhaps the Ordinary of Newgate[21] bids as fair for this office as any one. What should Mr. Bentham, sitting

----

[21] **Ordinary of Newgate** "the Chaplain of Newgate prison, whose duty it was to prepare condemned prisoners for death" (*Oxford English Dictionary*)

at ease in his arm-chair, composing his mind before he begins to write by a prelude on the organ, and looking out at a beautiful prospect when he is at a loss for an idea, know of the principles of action of rogues, outlaws, and vagabonds? No more than Montaigne of the motions of his cat! [22] If sanguine and tender-hearted philanthropists have set on foot an inquiry into the barbarity and the defects of penal laws, the practical improvements have been mostly suggested by reformed cut-throats, turnkeys, and thief-takers. What even can the Honourable House, who when the Speaker has pronounced the well-known, wished-for sounds, "That this house do now adjourn," retire, after voting a royal crusade or a loan of millions, to lie on down, and feed on plate in spacious palaces, know of what passes in the hearts of wretches in garrets and night-cellars, petty pilferers and marauders, who cut throats and pick pockets with their own hands? The thing is impossible. The laws of the country are, therefore, ineffectual and abortive, because they are made by the rich for the poor, by the wise for the ignorant, by the respectable and exalted in station for the very scum and refuse of the community. If Newgate would resolve itself into a committee of the whole Press-yard, with Jack Ketch at its head, aided by confidential persons from the county prisons or the Hulks,[23] and would make a clear breast, some *data* might be found out to proceed upon; but as it is, the *criminal mind* of the country is a book sealed, no one has been able to penetrate to the inside! Mr. Bentham, in his attempts to revise and amend our criminal jurisprudence, proceeds entirely on his fa-

---

[22] **Montaigne . . . cat** Montaigne's essay "Apology for Raimond de Sebonde." In attacking man's "presumptuous" belief that because animals do not possess human faculties they are necessarily stupid, Montaigne declares: "When I play with my cat, who knows whether I do not make her more sport than she makes me? we mutually divert one another with our monkey-tricks: if I have my hour to begin or to refuse, she also has hers" [23] **Press-yard** "name of a yard or court of old Newgate Prison . . . from which . . . capitally convicted prisoners started for the place of execution" (*Oxford English Dictionary*) **Jack Ketch** the hangman, from a notorious seventeenth-century executioner of that name **the Hulks** ships used as prisons

vourite principle of Utility. Convince highwaymen and housebreakers that it will be for their interest to reform, and they will reform and lead honest lives; according to Mr. Bentham. He says, "All men act from calculation, even madmen reason." [24] And, in our opinion, he might as well carry this maxim to Bedlam or St. Luke's,[25] and apply it to the inhabitants, as think to coerce or overawe the inmates of a gaol, or those whose practices make them candidates for that distinction, by the mere dry, detailed convictions of the understanding. Criminals are not to be influenced by reason; for it is of the very essence of crime to disregard consequences both to ourselves and others. You may as well preach philosophy to a drunken man, or to the dead, as to those who are under the instigation of any mischievous passion. A man is a drunkard, and you tell him he ought to be sober; he is debauched, and you ask him to reform; he is idle, and you recommend industry to him as his wisest course; he gambles, and you remind him that he may be ruined by this foible; he has lost his character, and you advise him to get into some reputable service or lucrative situation; vice becomes a habit with him, and you request him to rouse himself and shake it off; he is starving, and you warn him that if he breaks the law, he will be hanged. None of this reasoning reaches the mark it aims at. The culprit, who violates and suffers the vengeance of the laws, is not the dupe of ignorance, but the slave of passion, the victim of habit or necessity. To argue with strong passion, with inveterate habit, with desperate circumstances, is to talk to the winds. Clownish ignorance may indeed be dispelled, and taught better; but it is seldom that a criminal is not aware of the consequences of his act, or has not made up his mind to the alternative. They are, in general, *too knowing by half*. You tell a person of this stamp what is his interest; he says he does not care about his interest, or the world and he differ on that particular. But there is one point on which he

---

[24] From *An Introduction to the Principles of Morals and Legislation* (1789), the work in which Bentham first formulated the "principles of utility" [25] **Bedlam or St. Luke's** London insane asylums

must agree with them, namely, what *they* think of his conduct, and that is the only hold you have of him. A man may be callous and indifferent to what happens to himself; but he is never indifferent to public opinion, or proof against open scorn and infamy. Shame, then, not fear, is the sheet-anchor[26] of the law. He who is not afraid of being pointed at as a *thief*, will not mind a month's hard labour. He who is prepared to take the life of another, is already reckless of his own. But every one makes a sorry figure in the pillory; and the being launched from the New Drop[27] lowers a man in his own opinion. The lawless and violent spirit, who is hurried by head-strong self-will to break the laws, does not like to have the ground of pride and obstinacy struck from under his feet. This is what gives the *swells* of the metropolis such a dread of the *tread-mill*[28]—it makes them ridiculous. It must be confessed, that this very circumstance renders the reform of criminals nearly hopeless. It is the apprehension of being stigmatized by public opinion, the fear of what will be thought and said of them, that deters men from the violation of the laws, while their character remains unimpeached; but honour once lost, all is lost. The man can never be himself again! A citizen is like a soldier, a part of a machine, who submits to certain hardships, privations, and dangers, not for his own ease, pleasure, profit, or even conscience, but—*for shame*. What is it that keeps the machine together in either case? Not punishment or discipline, but sympathy. The soldier mounts the breach or stands in the trenches, the peasant hedges and ditches, or the mechanic plies his ceaseless task, because the one will not be called a *coward*, the other a *rogue*: but let the one turn deserter and the other vagabond, and there is an end of him. The grinding law of necessity, which is no other than a name, a breath, loses its force; he is no longer sustained by the good opinion of others, and he drops out of his place in 'so-

[26] **sheet-anchor** a large anchor for use in emergencies; by extension, anything in which one can place complete trust for its effectiveness [27] **New Drop** in Hazlitt's day the name for the trapdoor on which the condemned man stood for his hanging [28] **tread-mill** a revolving cylinder in which the prisoner was placed

ciety, a useless clog! Mr. Bentham takes a culprit, and puts him into what he calls a *Panopticon*,[29] that is, a sort of circular prison, with open cells, like a glass bee-hive. He sits in the middle, and sees all the other does. He gives him work to do, and lectures him if he does not do it. He takes liquor from him, and society and liberty; but he feeds and clothes him, and keeps him out of mischief; and when he has convinced him, by force and reason together, that this life is for his good, he turns him out upon the world a reformed man, and as confident of the success of his handy-work, as the shoemaker of that which he has just taken off the last, or the Parisian barber in Sterne, of the buckle of his wig. "Dip it in the ocean," said the perruquier, "and it will stand!" [30] But we doubt the durability of our projector's patchwork. Will our convert to the great principle of Utility work when he is from under Mr. Bentham's eye, because he was forced to work when under it? Will he keep sober, because he has been kept from liquor so long? Will he not return to loose company, because he has had the pleasure of sitting vis-à-vis with a philosopher of late? Will he not steal, now that his hands are untied? Will he not take the road, now that it is free to him? Will he not call his benefactor all the names he can set his tongue to, the moment his back is turned? All this is more than to be feared. The charm of criminal life, like that of savage life, consists in liberty, in hardship, in danger, and in the contempt of death, in one word, in extraordinary excitement; and he who has tasted of it, will no more return to regular habits of life, than a man will take to water after drinking brandy, or than a wild beast will give over hunting its prey. Miracles never cease, to be sure; but they are not to be had wholesale, or *to order*. Mr. Owen, who is another of these proprietors and patentees of reform, has lately got an American savage with him, whom

[29] In his *Panopticon, or, the Inspection House* (1791), Bentham described the appropriateness of this structure, not only for prisons, but also for poor-houses, industries, hospitals, and schools
[30] **the Parisian barber in Sterne . . . stand!** "The Wig. Paris," in A *Sentimental Journey* (1768) by **Laurence Sterne** (1713–68)

he carries about in great triumph and complacency, as an antithesis to his *New View of Society*,[31] and as winding up his reasoning to what it mainly wanted, an epigrammatic point. Does the benevolent visionary of the Lanark cotton-mills really think this *natural man* will act as a foil to his *artificial man?* Does he for a moment imagine that his *Address to the higher and middle classes*, with all its advantages of fiction, makes any thing like so interesting a romance as *Hunter's Captivity among the North American Indians?* [32] Has he any thing to show, in all the apparatus of New Lanark and its desolate monotony, to excite the thrill of imagination like the blankets made of wreaths of snow under which the wild wood-rovers bury themselves for weeks in winter? Or the skin of a leopard, which our hardy adventurer slew, and which served him for great-coat and bedding? Or the rattle-snake that he found by his side as a bedfellow? Or his rolling himself into a ball to escape from him? Or his suddenly placing himself against a tree to avoid being trampled to death by the herd of wild buffaloes, that came rushing on like the sound of thunder? Or his account of the huge spiders that prey on blue-bottles and gilded flies in green pathless forests; or of the great Pacific Ocean, that the natives look upon as the gulf that parts time from eternity, and that is to waft them to the spirits of their fathers? After all this, Mr. Hunter must find Mr. Owen and his parallelograms trite and flat, and will, we suspect, take an opportunity to escape from them!

Mr. Bentham's method of reasoning, though comprehensive and exact, labours under the defect of most systems—it is too *topical*. It includes every thing; but

[31] **Robert Owen** (1771–1858), social reformer and humanitarian *A New View of Society,* first published in 1813, was Owen's major statement on the reform of English industrial society, based on the "ideal community" he had established for his employees at the New Lanark (Scotland) textile mills [32] *Hunter's Captivity among the North American Indians* (1823), popular narrative by John Dunn Hunter (1798–1827), American "frontiersman." His account of childhood and adolescence spent among the Kickapoo, Kansas, and Osage Indians was a subject of considerable controversy in America, and was attacked as a complete fabrication

it includes every thing alike. It is rather like an inventory, than a valuation of different arguments. Every possible suggestion finds a place, so that the mind is distracted as much as enlightened by this perplexing accuracy. The exceptions seem as important as the rule. By attending to the minute, we overlook the great; and in summing up an account, it will not do merely to insist on the number of items without considering their amount. Our author's page presents a very nicely dove-tailed mosaic pavement of legal common-places. We slip and slide over its even surface without being arrested any where. Or his view of the human mind resembles a map, rather than a picture: the outline, the disposition is correct, but it wants colouring and relief. There is a technicality of manner, which renders his writings of more value to the professional inquirer than to the general reader. Again, his style is unpopular, not to say unintelligible. He writes a language of his own, that *darkens knowledge*. His works have been translated into French —they ought to be translated into English. People wonder that Mr. Bentham has not been prosecuted for the boldness and severity of some of his invectives. He might wrap up high treason in one of his inextricable periods, and it would never find its way into Westminster-Hall.[33] He is a kind of Manuscript author—he writes a cypher-hand, which the vulgar have no key to. The construction of his sentences is a curious frame-work with pegs and books to hang his thoughts upon, for his own use and guidance, but almost out of the reach of every body else. It is a barbarous philosophical jargon, with all the repetitions, parentheses, formalities, uncouth nomenclature and verbiage of law-Latin; and what makes it worse, it is not mere verbiage, but has a great deal of acuteness and meaning in it, which you would be glad to pick out if you could. In short, Mr. Bentham writes as if he was allowed but a single sentence to express his whole view of a subject in, and as if, should he omit a single circumstance or step of the argument, it would be lost to the world

[33] **Westminster-Hall** a building adjoining the Houses of Parliament; in Hazlitt's day, the site of the law courts

for ever, like an estate by a flaw in the title-deeds. This
is over-rating the importance of our own discoveries, and
mistaking the nature and object of language altogether.
Mr. Bentham has *acquired* this disability—it is not
natural to him. His admirable little work *On Usury*,[34]
published forty years ago, is clear, easy, and vigorous.
But Mr. Bentham has shut himself up since then "in
nook monastic," [35] conversing only with followers of his
own, or with "men of Ind," [36] and has endeavoured to
overlay his natural humour, sense, spirit, and style, with
the dust and cobwebs of an obscure solitude. The best
of it is, he thinks his present mode of expressing himself
perfect, and that whatever may be objected to his law
or logic, no one can find the least fault with the purity,
simplicity, and perspicuity of his style.

Mr. Bentham, in private life, is an amiable and ex-
emplary character. He is a little romantic, or so; and
has dissipated part of a handsome fortune in practical
speculations. He lends an ear to plausible projectors, and,
if he cannot prove them to be wrong in their premises
or their conclusions, thinks himself bound *in reason* to
stake his money on the venture. Strict logicians are
licensed visionaries. Mr. Bentham is half-brother to the
late Mr. Speaker Abbott—*Proh pudor!* [37] He was edu-
cated at Eton, and still takes our novices to task about a
passage in Homer, or a metre in Virgil. He was afterwards at the University, and he has described the scruples
of an ingenuous youthful mind about subscribing the
articles, in a passage in his *Church-of-Englandism*,[38] which
smacks of truth and honour both, and does one good to
read it in an age, when "to be honest" (or not to laugh
at the very idea of honesty) "is to be one man picked out

[34] *Defense of Usury*, written in 1787 [35] *As You Like It*, III, ii,
440–41 [36] *The Tempest*, II, ii, 61 [37] "Now Lord Colchester"
(Hazlitt's note) **Charles Abbot** (1757–1829), Tory politician
and Speaker of the House of Commons from 1802 to 1817
Proh pudor! "O Shame!" [38] **subscribing the articles** all university students of the time were required to assent to the Thirty-
nine Articles, a summary of Anglican religious belief *Church of
Englandism and its Cathechism Examined* was published in
1818

of ten thousand!" [39] Mr. Bentham relieves his mind sometimes, after the fatigue of study, by playing on a fine old
organ, and has a relish for Hogarth's prints. He turns
wooden utensils in a lathe for exercise, and fancies he
can turn man in the same manner. He has no great fond-
ness for poetry, and can hardly extract a moral out of
Shakspeare. His house is warmed and lighted by steam.
He is one of those who prefer the artificial to the natural
in most things, and think the mind of man omnipotent.
He has a great contempt for out-of-door prospects, for
green fields and trees, and is for referring every thing to
Utility. There is a little narrowness in this; for if all the
sources of satisfaction are taken away, what is to become
of utility itself? It is, indeed, the great fault of this able
and extraordinary man, that he has concentrated his
faculties and feelings too entirely on one subject and
pursuit, and has not "looked enough abroad into universality." [40]

January, 1824   1825

[39] *Hamlet*, II, ii, 178–79   [40] "Lord Bacon's Advancement of Learning" (Hazlitt's note)

Mr. Coleridge

The present is an age of talkers, and not of doers; and the reason is, that the world is growing old. We are so far advanced in the Arts and Sciences, that we live in retrospect, and dote on past achievements. The accumulation of knowledge has been so great, that we are lost in wonder at the height it has reached, instead of attempting to climb or add to it; while the variety of objects distracts and dazzles the looker-on. What *niche* remains unoccupied? What path untried? What is the use of doing anything, unless we could do better than all those who have gone before us? What hope is there of this? We are like those who have been to see some noble monument of art, who are content to admire without thinking of rivalling it; or like guests after a feast, who praise the hospitality of the donor "and thank the bounteous Pan" [1]—perhaps carrying away some trifling fragments; or like the spectators of a mighty battle, who still hear its sound afar off, and the clashing of armour and the neighing of the war-horse and the shout of victory is in their ears, like the rushing of innumerable waters!

Mr. Coleridge has "a mind reflecting ages past:" [2] his voice is like the echo of the congregated roar of the "dark rearward and abyss" [3] of thought. He who has seen a mouldering tower by the side of a chrystal lake, hid by the mist, but glittering in the wave below, may conceive the dim, gleaming, uncertain intelligence of his eye: he who has marked the evening clouds uprolled (a world of vapours), has seen the picture of his mind, unearthly, unsubstantial, with gorgeous tints and ever-varying forms—

[1] Milton's *Comus*, l. 175   [2] From laudatory verses prefacing the Second Folio of Shakespeare's Works, 1632   [3] Cf. *The Tempest*, I, ii, 50

That which was now a horse, even with a thought
The rack dislimns, and makes it indistinct
As water is in water.[4]

Our author's mind is (as he himself might express it)
tangential. There is no subject on which he has not
touched, none on which he has rested. With an understanding fertile, subtle, expansive, "quick, forgetive, ap-
prehensive," [5] beyond all living precedent, few traces of
it will perhaps remain. He lends himself to all impressions alike; he gives up his mind and liberty of thought
to none. He is a general lover of art and science, and
wedded to no one in particular. He pursues knowledge as
a mistress, with outstretched hands and winged speed;
but as he is about to embrace her, his Daphne turns—
alas! not to a laurel! [6] Hardly a speculation has been left
on record from the earliest time, but it is loosely folded up
in Mr. Coleridge's memory, like a rich, but somewhat
tattered piece of tapestry: we might add (with more
seeming than real extravagance), that scarce a thought
can pass through the mind of man, but its sound has at
some time or other passed over his head with rustling
pinions. On whatever question or author you speak, he is
prepared to take up the theme with advantage—from
Peter Abelard down to Thomas Moore, from the subtlest
metaphysics to the politics of the *Courier.*[7] There is no
man of genius, in whose praise he descants, but the critic
seems to stand above the author, and "what in him is
weak, to strengthen, what is low, to raise and support:" [8]
nor is there any work of genius that does not come out
of his hands like an illuminated Missal, sparkling even
in its defects. If Mr. Coleridge had not been the most
impressive talker of his age, he would probably have been
the finest writer; but he lays down his pen to make sure
of an auditor, and mortgages the admiration of posterity

---

[4] *Anthony and Cleopatra,* IV, xiv, 9–11   [5] *Henry IV, Part II,* IV,
iii, 106   [6] A reference to the myth of the nymph Daphne, who is
changed into a laurel tree to escape the embraces of the amorous
Apollo   [7] **Peter Abelard** (1079–1142), medieval preacher and
theologian   **Thomas Moore** (1779–1852), popular Irish poet
Courier, a London newspaper to which Coleridge contributed ir-
regularly over a number of years   [8] Cf. *Paradise Lost,* I, 22–23

for the stare of an idler. If he had not been a poet, he would have been a powerful logician; if he had not dipped his wing in the Unitarian controversy,[9] he might have soared to the very summit of fancy. But in writing verse, he is trying to subject the Muse to *transcendental* theories: in his abstract reasoning, he misses his way by strewing it with flowers. All that he has done of moment, he had done twenty years ago: since then, he may be said to have lived on the sound of his own voice. Mr. Coleridge is too rich in intellectual wealth, to need to task himself to any drudgery: he has only to draw the sliders of his imagination, and a thousand subjects expand before him, startling him with their brilliancy, or losing themselves in endless obscurity—

> "And by the force of blear illusion,
> They draw him on to his confusion." [10]

What is the little he could add to the stock, compared with the countless stores that lie about him, that he should stoop to pick up a name, or to polish an idle fancy? He walks abroad in the majesty of an universal understanding, eyeing the "rich strond," [11] or golden sky above him, and "goes sounding on his way," [12] in eloquent accents, uncompelled and free!

Persons of the greatest capacity are often those, who for this reason do the least; for surveying themselves from the highest point of view, amidst the infinite variety of the universe, their own share in it seems trifling, and scarce worth a thought, and they prefer the contemplation of all that is, or has been, or can be, to the making a coil [13] about doing what, when done, is no better than vanity. It is hard to concentrate all our attention and efforts on one pursuit, except from ignorance of others;

[9] **Unitarian controversy** a reference to the political and theological conflicts in the late eighteenth and early nineteenth centuries between the government and the Church of England, and those dissenters who argued for freedom of conscience and a belief in God the Father, rather than Christ or the Trinity, as the proper object of worship [10] *Macbeth*, III, v, 28–29 [11] *The Fairie Queene*, III, iv, 34 [12] Cf. Wordsworth's *Excursion*, III, 701 [13] **coil** fuss, much ado

and without this concentration of our faculties, no great progress can be made in any one thing. It is not merely that the mind is not capable of the effort; it does not think the effort worth making. Action is one; but thought is manifold. He whose restless eye glances through the wide compass of nature and art, will not consent to have "his own nothings monstered:" [14] but he must do this, before he can give his whole soul to them. The mind, after "letting contemplation have its fill," or

> "Sailing with supreme dominion
> Through the azure deep of air," [15]

sinks down on the ground, breathless, exhausted, powerless, inactive; or if it must have some vent to its feelings, seeks the most easy and obvious; is soothed by friendly flattery, lulled by the murmur of immediate applause, thinks as it were aloud, and babbles in its dreams! A scholar (so to speak) is a more disinterested and abstracted character than a mere author. The first looks at the numberless volumes of a library, and says, "All these are mine:" the other points to a single volume (perhaps it may be an immortal one) and says, "My name is written on the back of it." This is a puny and groveling ambition, beneath the lofty amplitude of Mr. Coleridge's mind. No, he revolves in his wayward soul, or utters to the passing wind, or discourses to his own shadow, things mightier and more various!—Let us draw the curtain, and unlock the shrine.

Learning rocked him in his cradle, and, while yet a child,

> "He lisped in numbers, for the numbers came.' [16]

At sixteen he wrote his *Ode on Chatterton*, and he still reverts to that period with delight, not so much as it relates to himself (for that string of his own early promise of fame rather jars than otherwise) but as exemplifying the youth of a poet. Mr. Coleridge talks of himself, with-

---

[14] *Coriolanus*, II, ii, 81 [15] John Dyer's *Grongar Hill* (1726), l. 26; and Gray's "Progress of Poesy," ll. 116–117 [16] Pope's *Epistle to Dr. Arbuthnot*, l. 128

out being an egotist, for in him the individual is always
merged in the abstract and general. He distinguished
himself at school and at the University by his knowledge
of the classics, and gained several prizes for Greek epi-
grams. How many men are there (great scholars, celebrated names in literature) who having done the same
thing in their youth, have no other idea all the rest of
their lives but of this achievement, of a fellowship and
dinner, and who, installed in academic honours, would
look down on our author as a mere strolling bard! At
Christ's Hospital,[17] where he was brought up, he was
the idol of those among his schoolfellows, who mingled
with their bookish studies the music of thought and of
humanity; and he was usually attended round the cloisters
by a group of these (inspiring and inspired) whose hearts,
even then, burnt within them as he talked, and where
the sounds yet linger to mock ELIA on his way, still
turning pensive to the past! One of the finest and rarest
parts of Mr. Coleridge's conversation, is when he ex-
patiates on the Greek tragedians (not that he is not well
acquainted, when he pleases, with the epic poets, or the
philosophers, or orators, or historians of antiquity)—on
the subtle reasonings and melting pathos of Euripides,
on the harmonious gracefulness of Sophocles, tuning his
love-laboured song, like sweetest warblings from a sacred
grove; on the high-wrought trumpet-tongued eloquence
of Æschylus, whose Prometheus, above all, is like an
Ode to Fate, and a pleading with Providence, his thoughts
being let loose as his body is chained on his solitary rock,
and his afflicted will (the emblem of mortality)

"Struggling in vain with ruthless destiny." [18]

As the impassioned critic speaks and rises in his theme,
you would think you heard the voice of the Man hated
by the Gods, contending with the wild winds as they
roar, and his eye glitters with the spirit of Antiquity!
   Next he was engaged with Hartley's tribes of mind,

[17] **Christ's Hospital** the London grammar school which Coleridge
attended from 1782 to 1791. Charles Lamb was a fellow-student
[18] Wordsworth's *Excursion*, VI, 557

"etherial braid, thought-woven,"—and he busied himself
for a year or two with vibrations and vibratiuncles and
the great law of association that binds all things in its
mystic chain, and the doctrine of Necessity (the mild
teacher of Charity) and the Millennium,[19] anticipative
of a life to come—and he plunged deep into the controversy on Matter and Spirit, and, as an escape from Dr.
Priestley's Materialism,[20] where he felt himself imprisoned
by the logician's spell, like Ariel in the cloven pine-tree,[21]
he became suddenly enamoured of Bishop Berkeley's fairy-
world,[22] and used in all companies to build the universe,
like a brave poetical fiction, of fine words—and he was
deep-read in Malebranche,[23] and in Cudworth's Intellectual System[24] (a huge pile of learning, unwieldy, enor-

---

[19] **David Hartley** (1705–57), philosopher, author of the influential *Observations on Man* (1749). The first volume explained
the operation of the mind and the development of human thought
by the association of ideas and by vibrations in the brain from the
sensible impressions of external objects. The second volume dis-
cussed matters of religion and morality   **"etherial braid, thought-
woven"** cf. William Collins' "Ode to Evening" (1746), l. 7
[20] **Joseph Priestley** (1733–1804), important scientist and controversial political and religious dissenter. In various writings, he advanced the "atheistic" doctrine that man's soul was merely an
activity or property of his material nature   [21] **Ariel in the cloven
pine-tree** *The Tempest*, I, ii, 269–93   [22] "Mr. Coleridge named
his eldest son (the writer of some beautiful Sonnets) after Hartley, and the second after Berkeley. The third was called Derwent,
after the river of that name. Nothing can be more characteristic
of his mind than this circumstance. All his ideas indeed are like
a river, flowing on for ever, and still murmuring as it flows, dis-
charging its waters and still replenished—

  'And so by many winding nooks it strays,
  With willing sport to the wild ocean!' "

(Hazlitt's note)   **George Berkeley** (1685–1753), clergyman and
idealistic philosopher, who argued that spirit and mind were the
only sources of reality   'And so . . . ocean!' Cf. *Two Gentlemen
of Verona*, II, vii, 31–32   [23] **Nicolas Malebranche** (1638–1715),
French philosopher and follower of Descartes   [24] **Ralph Cudworth**
(1617–88), English philosopher and theologian, one of the Cambridge Platonists. His major philosophic work *The True Intellectual System of the Universe* (1678) was an elaborate refutation
of atheism, including an examination of pagan religious beliefs

mous) and in Lord Brook's hieroglyphic theories,[25] and in Bishop Butler's Sermons,[26] and in the Duchess of Newcastle's fantastic folios,[27] and in Clarke and South and Tillotson,[28] and all the fine thinkers and masculine reasoners of that age—and Leibnitz's *Pre-established Harmony*[29] reared its arch above his head, like the rainbow in the cloud, convenanting with the hopes of man—and then he fell plump, ten thousand fathoms down (but his wings saved him harmless) into the *hortus siccus* of Dissent,[30] where he pared religion down to the standard of reason, and stripped faith of mystery, and preached Christ crucified and the Unity of the Godhead, and so dwelt for a while in the spirit with John Huss and Jerome of Prague and Socinus and old John Zisca,[31] and ran through Neal's History of the Puritans, and Calamy's Non-Conformists' Memorial,[32] having like thoughts and passions

[25] Fulke Greville, **first Baron Brooke** (1554–1628), poet and dramatist, friend of Sir Philip Sidney. His works are notable for their stylistic and philosophic complexity [26] **Joseph Butler** (1692–1752), preacher and moralist, whose *Fifteen Sermons* (1726) and *The Analogy of Religion* (1736) were influential religious texts into the nineteenth century [27] Margaret Cavendish, **Duchess of Newcastle** (1624?–74), author of various works in poetry and prose, often embodying eccentric philosophic and scientific speculations [28] **Samuel Clarke** (1675–1729), **Robert South** (1634–1716), **John Tillotson** (1630–94), leading theologians and preachers of their time [29] **Leibnitz's *Pre-established Harmony*** the highly optimistic philosophic doctrines of Gottfried Wilhelm Leibnitz (1646–1716), who argued that the dynamic forces of matter and mind function in a perfect order and relationship instituted by God, to produce "the best of all possible worlds" [30] ***hortus siccus*** of Dissent, "withered garden", referring to Coleridge's period of Unitarian engagement [31] **John Huss** (1369?–1415) **Jerome of Prague** (d. 1416) **Socinus** Lelio Francesco Maria Sozini (1525–62) or Fausto Paolo Sozzini (1539–1604), early religious reformers and dissenters from Roman Catholicism **Zisca** John Zizka (d. 1424), military leader of the Hussite armies in Bohemia against the German-Catholic forces [32] **Daniel Neal** (1678–1743) and **Edmund Calamy** (1671–1732), dissenting ministers and leading historians of the non-conformist movement. Neal's *History of the Puritans* was published between 1732 and 1738. Calamy wrote several publications on the life and times of Richard Baxter, a famous Presbyterian author and preacher of the seventeenth century; these works were brought together in 1775 under the title *The Non-Conformists' Memorial*

with them—but then Spinoza[33] became his God, and he took up the vast chain of being in his hand, and the round world became the centre and the soul of all things in some shadowy sense, forlorn of meaning, and around him he beheld the living traces and the sky-pointing proportions of the mighty Pan—but poetry redeemed him from this spectral philosophy, and he bathed his heart in beauty, and gazed at the golden light of heaven, and drank of the spirit of the universe, and wandered at eve by fairy-stream or fountain,

> "——When he saw nought but beauty,
> When he heard the voice of that Almighty One
> In every breeze that blew, or wave that mur-
> mured——." [34]

and wedded with truth in Plato's shade, and in the writings of Proclus and Plotinus[35] saw the ideas of things in the eternal mind, and unfolded all mysteries with the Schoolmen and fathomed the depths of Duns Scotus and Thomas Aquinas,[36] and entered the third heaven with Jacob Behmen,[37] and walked hand in hand with Swedenborg[38] through the pavilions of the New Jerusalem, and sung his faith in the promise and in the word in his *Religious Musings*[39]—and lowering himself from that dizzy height, poised himself on Milton's wings, and spread out his thoughts in charity with the glad prose of Jeremy Taylor,[40] and wept over Bowles's Sonnets,[41] and studied

[33] **Benedictus de Spinoza** (1632–77), Dutch philosopher, who advanced the "pantheistic" doctrine of the unity and coexistence of God, nature, and the mind as "one infinite substance" [34] Coleridge's tragedy, *Remorse* (1813), IV, ii, 101–03 [35] **Proclus** (410?–85) and **Plotinus** (204–70), leading formulators of Neoplatonic philosophy [36] **Duns Scotus** (1265?–1308) and **Thomas Aquinas** (1225?–1274), leading spokesmen of the Scholastic philosophy of the middle ages [37] **Jacob Behmen** (1575–1624), German religious mystic and writer [38] **Emanuel Swedenborg** (1688–1772), Swedish scientist and mystic [39] **Religious Musings** a "desultory poem" by Coleridge, published in 1796 [40] **Jeremy Taylor** (1613–67), clergyman and writer of works on religion and morality, famous models of English prose style [41] **William Lisle Bowles** (1762–1850), whose *Sonnets* (1789) had a considerable influence on the first generation of English Romantic poets

Cowper's blank verse, and betook himself to Thomson's Castle of Indolence,[42] and sported with the wits of Charles the Second's days and of Queen Anne, and relished Swift's style and that of the John Bull (Arbuthnot's we mean, not Mr. Croker's),[43] and dallied with the British Essayists and Novelists, and knew all qualities of more modern writers with a learned spirit, Johnson, and Goldsmith, and Junius,[44] and Burke, and Godwin,[45] and the Sorrows of Werter,[46] and Jean Jacques Rousseau, and Voltaire, and Marivaux,[47] and Crebillon, and thousands more—now "laughed with Rabelais in his easy chair"[48] or pointed to Hogarth, or afterwards dwelt on Claude's classic scenes, or spoke with rapture of Raphael, and compared the women at Rome to figures that had walked out of his pictures, or visited the Oratory at Pisa, and described the works of Giotto and Ghirlandaio[49] and Massaccio, and gave the moral of the picture of the Triumph of Death,[50] where the beggars and the wretched invoke his dreadful dart, but the rich and mighty of the earth quail and shrink before it; and in that land of siren sights and sounds, saw a dance of peasant girls, and was charmed with lutes and gondolas,—or wandered into

[42] **Thomson's Castle of Indolence** a poem in Spenserian stanzas by James Thomson, published in 1748   [43] **John Arbuthnot** (1667–1735), physician and writer, associate of Swift and Pope; his *History of John Bull*, a political satire, was published in 1712 **John Wilson Croker** (1780–1857), Tory politician and journalist, was erroneously thought to have been the editor of *John Bull*, a virulently anti-Whig newspaper first published in 1820   [44] **Junius** the pseudonym of the author of controversial letters, published 1769–1771, sharply attacking George III and his government   [45] **William Godwin** (1756–1836), philosopher and novelist, whose *Enquiry concerning Political Justice* (1793) was one of the most influential publications of the time   [46] **Sorrows of Werther** Goethe's famous sentimental novel, first published in 1774   [47] **Pierre Carlet de Chamblain de Marivaux** (1688–1763), popular French writer of sentimental novels and plays [48] Cf. Pope's *Dunciad*, I, 22   [49] **Giotto** (Ambrogio di Bondone) (1266?–1337), famous painter of religious frescoes and architect; early master of the Florentine school **Domenico Ghirlandaio** (1449?–94), Florentine painter and master of Michelangelo [50] **Triumph of Death** a famous allegorical fresco in the Campo Santo at Pisa, dating from the fourteenth century

Germany and lost himself in the labyrinths of the Hartz
Forest and of the Kantean philosophy, and amongst the
cabalistic names of Fichtè and Schelling and Lessing,[51]
and God knows who—this was long after, but all the
former while, he had nerved his heart and filled his eyes
with tears, as he hailed the rising orb of liberty, since
quenched in darkness and in blood, and had kindled his
affections at the blaze of the French Revolution, and
sang for joy when the towers of the Bastile and the proud
places of the insolent and the oppressor fell, and would
have floated his bark, freighted with fondest fancies, across
the Atlantic wave with Southey and others to seek for
peace and freedom—

> "In Philharmonia's undivided dale!" [52]

Alas! "Frailty, thy name is *Genius*!" [53]—What is become
of all this mighty heap of hope, of thought, of learning,
and humanity? It has ended in swallowing doses of
oblivion[54] and in writing paragraphs in the *Courier*.—
Such, and so little is the mind of man!

It is not to be supposed that Mr. Coleridge could
keep on at the rate he set off; he could not realize all
he knew or thought, and less could not fix his desultory
ambition; other stimulants supplied the place, and kept
up the intoxicating dream, the fever and the madness of
his early impressions. Liberty (the philosopher's and the
poet's bride) had fallen a victim, meanwhile, to the
murderous practices of the hag, Legitimacy. Proscribed by
court-hirelings, too romantic for the herd of vulgar poli-

[51] **wandered into Germany . . . Lessing** referring to Coleridge's
visit to Germany in 1798–99 **cabalistic** mystical, occult. The
leading German idealistic philosophers, **Johann Gottlieb Fichte**
(1762–1814) and **Friedrich Wilhelm Joseph von Schelling**
(1775–1854); and the famous critic and dramatist **Gotthold
Ephraim Lessing** (1729–81) [52] Hazlitt quotes from Coleridge's
poem "To the Rev. W. J. Hort" (1796), referring to Pantisoc-
racy, a scheme devised by Coleridge and the poet **Robert Southey**
(1774–1843) for an ideal community on the banks of the
Susquehanna in Pennsylvania [53] Cf. *Hamlet*, I, ii, 146 [54] **swallowing doses of oblivion** a reference to Coleridge's addiction to
opium

ticians, our enthusiast stood at bay, and at last turned on the pivot of a subtle casuistry to the *unclean side*: but his discursive reason would not let him trammel himself into a poet-laureate or stamp-distributor,[55] and he stopped, ere he had quite passed that well-known "bourne from whence no traveller returns" [56]—and so has sunk into torpid, uneasy repose, tantalized by useless resources, haunted by vain imaginings, his lips idly moving, but his heart for ever still, or, as the shattered chords vibrate of themselves, making melancholy music to the ear of memory! Such is the fate of genius in an age, when in the unequal contest with sovereign wrong, every man is ground to powder who is not either a born slave, or who does not willingly and at once offer up the yearnings of humanity and the dictates of reason as a welcome sacrifice to besotted prejudice and loathsome power.

Of all Mr. Coleridge's productions, the *Ancient Mariner* is the only one that we could with confidence put into any person's hands, on whom we wished to impress a favourable idea of his extraordinary powers. Let whatever other objections be made to it, it is unquestionably a work of genius—of wild, irregular, overwhelming imagination, and has that rich, varied movement in the verse, which gives a distant idea of the lofty or changeful tones of Mr. Coleridge's voice. In the *Christabel*, there is one splendid passage on divided friendship.[57] The *Translation of Schiller's Wallenstein*[58] is also a masterly production in its kind, faithful and spirited. Among his smaller pieces there are occasional bursts of pathos and fancy, equal to what we might expect from him; but these form the exception, and not the rule. Such, for instance, is his affecting Sonnet to the author of the Robbers.

---

[55] **poet-laureate or stamp-distributor** referring to Southey and Wordsworth, who renounced the revolutionary principles of their early years and became supporters of the policies of the British government against the French. In 1813, Southey was named laureate, and Wordsworth was appointed Distributor of Stamps for the County of Westmoreland [56] *Hamlet*, III, i, 79–80 [57] **one splendid passage on divided friendship** ll. 408–426 [58] *Translation of Schiller's Wallenstein* published in 1800

Schiller! that hour I would have wish'd to die,
 If through the shudd'ring midnight I had sent
 From the dark dungeon of the tower time-rent,
That fearful voice, a famish'd father's cry—
That in no after-moment aught less vast
 Might stamp me mortal! A triumphant shout
 Black horror scream'd, and all her goblin rout
From the more with'ring scene diminish'd pass'd.
Ah! Bard tremendous in sublimity!
 Could I behold thee in thy loftier mood,
Wand'ring at eve, with finely frenzied eye,
 Beneath some vast old tempest-swinging wood!
 Awhile, with mute awe gazing, I would brood,
Then weep aloud in a wild ecstasy.

His Tragedy, entitled *Remorse*, is full of beautiful and striking passages, but it does not place the author in the first rank of dramatic writers. But if Mr. Coleridge's works do not place him in that rank, they injure instead of conveying a just idea of the man, for he himself is certainly in the first class of general intellect.

If our author's poetry is inferior to his conversation, his prose is utterly abortive. Hardly a gleam is to be found in it of the brilliancy and richness of those stores of thought and language that he pours out incessantly, when they are lost like drops of water in the ground. The principal work, in which he has attempted to embody his general views of things, is the FRIEND,[59] of which, though it contains some noble passages and fine trains of thought, prolixity and obscurity are the most frequent characteristics.

No two persons can be conceived more opposite in character or genius than the subject of the present and of the preceding sketch. Mr. Godwin, with less natural capacity, and with fewer acquired advantages, by concentrating his mind on some given object, and doing what he had to do with all his might, has accomplished

[59] the FRIEND a journal of miscellaneous articles on politics, literature, and morals, originally published in 1809–10, and collected in book form in 1812

much, and will leave more than one monument of a powerful intellect behind him; Mr. Coleridge, by dissipating his, and dallying with every subject by turns, has done little or nothing to justify to the world or to posterity, the high opinion which all who have ever heard him converse, or known him intimately, with one accord entertain of him. Mr. Godwin's faculties have kept at home, and plied their task in the workshop of the brain, diligently and effectually: Mr. Coleridge's have gossiped away their time, and gadded about from house to house, as if life's business were to melt the hours in listless talk. Mr. Godwin is intent on a subject, only as it concerns himself and his reputation; he works it out as a matter of duty, and discards from his mind whatever does not forward his main object as impertinent and vain. Mr. Coleridge, on the other hand, delights in nothing but episodes and digressions, neglects whatever he undertakes to perform, and can act only on spontaneous impulses, without object or method. "He cannot be constrained by mastery." [60] While he should be occupied with a given pursuit, he is thinking of a thousand other things; a thousand tastes, a thousand objects tempt him, and distract his mind, which keeps open house, and entertains all comers; and after being fatigued and amused with morning calls from idle visitors, finds the day consumed and its business unconcluded. Mr. Godwin, on the contrary, is somewhat exclusive and unsocial in his habits of mind, entertains no company but what he gives his whole time and attention to, and wisely writes over the doors of his understanding, his fancy, and his senses— "No admittance except on business." He has none of that fastidious refinement and false delicacy, which might lead him to balance between the endless variety of modern attainments. He does not throw away his life (nor a single half-hour of it) in adjusting the claims of different accomplishments, and in choosing between them or making himself master of them all. He sets about his task, (whatever it may be) and goes through it with spirit and fortitude. He has the happiness to think an

[60] Cf. Wordsworth's *Excursion*, VI, 163–64

author the greatest character in the world, and himself
the greatest author in it.[61] Mr. Coleridge, in writing an
harmonious stanza, would stop to consider whether there
was not more grace and beauty in a *Pas de trois,* and
would not proceed till he had resolved this question by
a chain of metaphysical reasoning without end. Not so
Mr. Godwin. That is best to him, which he can do best.
He does not waste himself in vain aspirations and effeminate sympathies. He is blind, deaf, insensible to all
but the trump of Fame. Plays, operas, painting, music,
ball-rooms, wealth, fashion, titles, lords, ladies, touch
him not—all these are no more to him than to the
magician in his cell, and he writes on to the end of the
chapter, through good report and evil report. *Pingo in
eternitatem*[62]—is his motto. He neither envies nor ad-
mires what others are, but is contented to be what he is,
and strives to do the utmost he can. Mr. Coleridge has
flirted with the Muses as with a set of mistresses: Mr.
Godwin has been married twice, to Reason and to
Fancy,[63] and has to boast no short-lived progeny by each.
So to speak, he has *valves* belonging to his mind, to
regulate the quantity of gas admitted into it, so that like
the bare, unsightly, but well-compacted steam-vessel, it
cuts its liquid way, and arrives at its promised end: while
Mr. Coleridge's bark, "taught with the little nautilus to
sail," [64] the sport of every breath, dancing to every wave,

"Youth at its prow, and Pleasure at its helm," [65]

flutters its gaudy pennons in the air, glitters in the sun,
but we wait in vain to hear of its arrival in the destined
harbour. Mr. Godwin, with less variety and vividness,

[61] **He has the happiness . . . author in it**   modelled on a remark
by Parson Adams in Fielding's *Joseph Andrews* (1742), Book III,
Chapter 5   [62] "I paint for eternity," a remark attributed to the
Greek painter Zeuxis in Reynolds' Third Discourse   [63] **Mr. God-
win . . . Reason and to Fancy**   referring to Godwin's intellec-
tual career as philosopher and novelist. In private life, Godwin
had been married twice: to Mary Wollstonecraft, author of the
Vindication of the Rights of Woman (1792), and mother of
Shelley's wife Mary; and to Mrs. Mary Clairmont   [64] Pope's
Essay on Man, III, 177   [65] Gray's "The Bard," l. 74

with less subtlety and susceptibility both of thought and feeling, has had firmer nerves, a more determined purpose, a more comprehensive grasp of his subject, and the results are as we find them. Each has met with his reward: for justice has, after all, been done to the pretensions of each; and we must, in all cases, use means to ends!

It was a misfortune to any man of talent to be born in the latter end of the last century. Genius stopped the way of Legitimacy, and therefore it was to be abated, crushed, or set aside as a nuisance. The spirit of the monarchy was at variance with the spirit of the age. The flame of liberty, the light of intellect, was to be extinguished with the sword—or with slander, whose edge is sharper than the sword. The war between power and reason was carried on by the first of these abroad—by the last at home. No quarter was given (then or now) by the Government-critics, the authorised censors of the press, to those who followed the dictates of independence, who listened to the voice of the tempter, Fancy. Instead of gathering fruits and flowers, immortal fruits and amaranthine flowers, they soon found themselves beset not only by a host of prejudices, but assailed by all the engines of power, by nicknames, by lies, by all the arts of malice, interest, and hypocrisy, without a possibility of their defending themselves "from the pelting of the pitiless storm," [66] that poured down upon them from the strong-holds of corruption and authority. The philosophers, the dry abstract reasoners, submitted to this reverse pretty well, and armed themselves with patience "as with triple steel," [67] to bear discomfiture, persecution, and disgrace. But the poets, the creatures of sympathy, could not stand the frowns both of king and people. They did not like to be shut out when places and pensions, when the critic's praises, and the laurel-wreath were about to be distributed. They did not stomach being *sent to Coventry*,[68] and Mr. Coleridge sounded a retreat for them by the help of casuistry, and a musical voice.—"His words were hollow, but they pleased the

[66] *King Lear*, III, iv, 29   [67] *Paradise Lost*, II, 569   [68] *sent to Coventry* proverbial expression for social disgrace

ear" [69] of his friends of the Lake School, who turned back disgusted and panic-struck from the dry desert of unpopularity, like Hassan the camel-driver,

"And curs'd the hour, and curs'd the luckless day,
    When first from Shiraz' walls they bent their way." [70]

They are safely inclosed there, but Mr. Coleridge did not enter with them; pitching his tent upon the barren waste without, and having no abiding place nor city of refuge!

1825

[69] Cf. *Paradise Lost*, II, 112–17   [70] William Collins' Second Persian Eclogue, "Hassan; or, the Camel Driver" (1742)

On Going a Journey

One of the pleasantest things in the world is going a journey; but I like to go by myself. I can enjoy society in a room; but out of doors, nature is company enough for me. I am then never less alone than when alone.

"The fields his study, nature was his books." [1]

I cannot see the wit of walking and talking at the same time. When I am in the country, I wish to vegetate like the country. I am not for criticising hedge-rows and black cattle. I go out of town in order to forget the town and all that is in it. There are those who for this purpose go to watering-places, and carry the metropolis with them. I like more elbow-room, and fewer incumbrances. I like solitude, when I give myself up to it, for the sake of solitude; nor do I ask for

———"a friend in my retreat,
Whom I may whisper solitude is sweet." [2]

The soul of a journey is liberty; perfect liberty, to think, feel, do just as one pleases. We go a journey chiefly to be free of all impediments and of all inconveniences; to leave ourselves behind, much more to get rid of others. It is because I want a little breathing-space to muse on indifferent matters, where Contemplation

"May plume her feathers and let grow her wings,
That in the various bustle of resort
Were all too ruffled, and sometimes impair'd," [3]

that I absent myself from the town for a while, without feeling at a loss the moment I am left by myself. Instead

[1] Robert Bloomfield's *The Farmer's Boy* (1800), "Spring," l. 32
[2] Cowper's "Retirement" (1782), ll. 741–42 [3] Milton's *Comus*, ll. 378–80

of a friend in a post-chaise or in a tilbury, to exchange
good things with, and vary the same stale topics over
again, for once let me have a truce with impertinence.
Give me the clear blue sky over my head, and the green
turf beneath my feet, a winding road before me, and a
three hours' march to dinner—and then to thinking!
It is hard if I cannot start some game on these lone
heaths. I laugh, I run, I leap, I sing for joy. From the
point of yonder rolling cloud, I plunge into my past
being, and revel there, as the sun-burnt Indian plunges
headlong into the wave that wafts him to his native shore.
Then long-forgotten things, like "sunken wrack and sum-
less treasuries," [4] burst upon my eager sight, and I begin
to feel, think, and be myself again. Instead of an awk-
ward silence, broken by attempts at wit or dull common-
places, mine is that undisturbed silence of the heart
which alone is perfect eloquence. No one likes puns, alliterations, antitheses, argument, and analysis better than
I do; but I sometimes had rather be without them.
"Leave, oh, leave me to my repose!" [5] I have just now
other business in hand, which would seem idle to you,
but is with me "the very stuff of the conscience." [6] Is
not this wild rose sweet without a comment? Does not
this daisy leap to my heart, set in its coat of emerald?
Yet if I were to explain to you the circumstance that
has so endeared it to me, you would only smile. Had I
not better then keep it to myself, and let it serve me
to brood over, from here to yonder craggy point, and
from thence onward to the far-distant horizon? I should
be but bad company all that way, and therefore prefer
being alone. I have heard it said that you may, when the
moody fit comes on, walk or ride on by yourself, and
indulge your reveries. But this looks like a breach of
manners, a neglect of others, and you are thinking all the
time that you ought to rejoin your party. "Out upon
such half-faced fellowship," [7] say I. I like to be either
entirely to myself, or entirely at the disposal of others;
to talk or be silent, to walk or sit still, to be sociable or

[4] Shakespeare's *Henry V*, I, ii, 165   [5] Refrain in Gray's "The
Descent of Odin" (1768)   [6] *Othello*, I, ii, 2   [7] *Henry IV, Part I*,
I, iii, 208

solitary. I was pleased with an observation of Mr. Cobbett's, that "he thought it a bad French custom to drink our wine with our meals, and that an Englishman ought to do only one thing at a time." So I cannot talk and think, or indulge in melancholy musing and lively conversation by fits and starts. "Let me have a companion of my way," says Sterne, "were it but to remark how the shadows lengthen as the sun goes down." It is beautifully said: but in my opinion, this continual comparing of notes interferes with the involuntary impression of things upon the mind, and hurts the sentiment. If you only hint what you feel in a kind of dumb show, it is insipid: if you have to explain it, it is making a toil of a pleasure. You cannot read the book of nature, without being perpetually put to the trouble of translating it for the benefit of others. I am for the synthetical method on a journey, in preference to the analytical. I am content to lay in a stock of ideas then, and to examine and anatomise them afterwards. I want to see my vague notions float like the down of the thistle before the breeze, and not to have them entangled in the briars and thorns of controversy. For once, I like to have it all my own way; and this is impossible, unless you are alone, or in such company as I do not covet. I have no objection to argue a point with any one for twenty miles of measured road, but not for pleasure. If you remark the scent of a beanfield crossing the road, perhaps your fellow-traveller has no smell. If you point to a distant object, perhaps he is short-sighted, and has to take out his glass to look at it. There is a feeling in the air, a tone in the colour of a cloud which hits your fancy, but the effect of which you are unprepared to account for. There is then no sympathy, but an uneasy craving after it, and a dissatisfaction which pursues you on the way, and in the end probably produces ill humour. Now I never quarrel with myself, and take all my own conclusions for granted till I find it necessary to defend them against objections. It is not merely that you may not be of accord on the objects and circumstances that present themselves before you—they may recall a number of ideas, and lead to associations too delicate and refined to be possibly communicated to others. Yet these I love to cherish, and sometimes still fondly clutch them, when I can escape from the throng to do so. To give way to our feelings before company, seems extravagance or affectation; on the other hand, to have to unravel this mystery of our being at every turn, and to make others take an equal interest in it (otherwise the end is not answered) is a task to which few are competent. We must "give it an understanding, but no tongue." [8] My old friend Coleridge, however, could do both. He could go on in the most delightful explanatory way over hill and dale, a summer's day, and convert a landscape into a didactic poem or a Pindaric ode. "He talked far above singing." [9] If I could so clothe my ideas in sounding and flowing words, I might perhaps wish to have some one with me to admire the swelling theme; or I could be more content, were it possible for me still to hear his echoing voice in the woods of All-Foxden. [10] They had "that fine madness in them which our first poets had;" [11] and if they could have been caught by some rare instrument, would have breathed such strains as the following:

> ———"Here be woods as green
> As any, air likewise as fresh and sweet
> As when smooth Zephyrus plays on the fleet
> Face of the curled stream, with flow'rs as many
> As the young spring gives, and as choice as any;
> Here be all new delights, cool streams, and wells,
> Arbours o'ergrown with woodbine, caves and dells;
> Choose where thou wilt, while I sit by and sing,
> Or gather rushes to make many a ring
> For thy long fingers; tell thee tales of love,
> How the pale Phoebe, hunting in a grove,
> First saw the boy Endymion, from whose eyes
> She took eternal fire that never dies;
> How she convey'd him softly in a sleep,

---

[8] *Hamlet*, I, ii, 250 [9] Beaumont and Fletcher's tragic-comedy, *Philaster*, V, v [10] **All-Foxden** in Somersetshire, where Wordsworth and Coleridge wrote *Lyrical Ballads* (1798). Hazlitt had paid a memorable visit to them in the early summer of that year [11] Cf. "Elegy to my Most Dearely-loved Friend Henery Reynolds Esquire" (1627), ll. 109–10, by Michael Drayton

His temples bound with poppy, to the steep
Head of old Latmos, where she stoops each night,
Gilding the mountain with her brother's light,
To kiss her sweetest."——
                              FAITHFUL SHEPHERDESS [12]

Had I words and images at command like these, I would
attempt to wake the thoughts that lie slumbering on
golden ridges in the evening clouds: but at the sight
of nature my fancy, poor as it is, droops and closes up
its leaves, like flowers at sunset. I can make nothing out
on the spot:—I must have time to collect myself.

In general, a good thing spoils out-of-door prospects:
it should be reserved for Table-talk. L——[13] is for this
reason, I take it, the worst company in the world out of
doors; because he is the best within. I grant, there is one
subject on which it is pleasant to talk on a journey; and
that is, what one shall have for supper when we get to
our inn at night. The open air improves this sort of conversation or friendly altercation, by setting a keener edge
on appetite. Every mile of the road heightens the flavour
of the viands we expect at the end of it. How fine it is
to enter some old town, walled and turreted, just at the
approach of night-fall, or to come to some straggling
village, with the lights streaming through the surround-
ing gloom; and then after inquiring for the best enter-
tainment that the place affords, to "take one's ease at
one's inn!" [14] These eventful moments in our lives are in
fact too precious, too full of solid, heart-felt happiness
to be frittered and dribbled away in imperfect sympathy.
I would have them all to myself, and drain them to the
last drop: they will do to talk of or to write about afterwards. What a delicate speculation it is, after drinking
whole goblets of tea,

"The cups that cheer, but not inebriate," [15]

and letting the fumes ascend into the brain, to sit considering what we shall have for supper—eggs and a

---

[12] A pastoral play by John Fletcher   [13] Charles Lamb   [14] *Henry
IV, Part I*, III, iii, 93   [15] Cowper's *The Task*, IV, 39–40

rasher, a rabbit smothered in onions, or an excellent veal-cutlet! Sancho in such a situation once fixed upon cow-heel; and his choice, though he could not help it, is not to be disparaged. Then, in the intervals of pictured scenery and Shandean contemplation,[16] to catch the preparation and the stir in the kitchen—*Procul, O procul este profani*![17] These hours are sacred to silence and to musing, to be treasured up in the memory, and to feed the source of smiling thoughts hereafter. I would not waste them in idle talk; or if I must have the integrity of fancy broken in upon, I would rather it were by a stranger than a friend. A stranger takes his hue and character from the time and place; he is a part of the furniture and costume of an inn. If he is a Quaker, or from the West Riding of Yorkshire, so much the better. I do not even try to sympathise with him, and he *breaks no squares*.[18] I associate nothing with my travelling companion but present objects and passing events. In his ignorance of me and my affairs, I in a manner forget myself. But a friend reminds one of other things, rips up old grievances, and destroys the abstraction of the scene. He comes in ungraciously between us and our imaginary character. Something is dropped in the course of conversation that gives a hint of your profession and pursuits; or from having some one with you that knows the less sublime portions of your history, it seems that other people do. You are no longer a citizen of the world: but your "unhoused free condition is put into circumscription and confine."[19] The *incognito* of an inn is one of its striking privileges— "lord of one's-self, uncumber'd with a name."[20] Oh! it is great to shake off the trammels of the world and of public opinion—to lose our importunate, tormenting, everlasting personal identity in the elements of nature, and become the creature of the moment, clear of all ties—to hold to the universe only by a

[16] **Shandean contemplation** referring to the apparently random and bizarre speculations and associations of ideas that define the main characters in Sterne's *Tristram Shandy* (1760–67)   [17] "O ye profane, be far, far away!" Virgil's *Aeneid*, VI, 258   [18] *breaks no squares* proverbial expression, meaning "makes no difference"   [19] *Othello*, I, ii. 26–27   [20] Dryden's "To my Honour'd Kinsman, John Driden" (1700) l. 18

dish of sweet-breads, and to owe nothing but the score of the evening—and no longer seeking for applause and meeting with contempt, to be known by no other title than the *Gentleman in the parlour!* One may take one's choice of all characters in this romantic state of uncertainty as to one's real pretensions, and become indefinitely respectable and negatively right-worshipful. We baffle prejudice and disappoint conjecture; and from being so to others, begin to be objects of curiosity and wonder even to ourselves. We are no more those hackneyed common-places that we appear in the world: an inn restores us to the level of nature, and quits scores with society! I have certainly spent some enviable hours at inns—sometimes when I have been left entirely to myself, and have tried to solve some metaphysical problem, as once at Witham-Common, where I found out the proof that likeness is not a case of the association of ideas—at other times, when there have been pictures in the room, as at St. Neot's[21] (I think it was) where I first met with Gribelin's engravings of the Cartoons,[22] into which I entered at once; and at a little inn on the borders of Wales, where there happened to be hanging some of Westall's drawings,[23] which I compared triumphantly (for a theory that I had, not for the admired artist) with the figure of a girl who had ferried me over the Severn,[24] standing up in the boat between me and the fading twilight—at other times I might mention luxuriating in books with a peculiar interest in this way, as I remember sitting up half the night to read Paul and Virginia, which I picked up at an inn at Bridgewater,[25] after being drenched in the rain all day; and at the same place I got through two volumes of Madame D'Arblay's Camilla.[26] It was on the

[21] St. Neot's town in Huntingtonshire [22] Simon Gribelin (1661–1733), French-English engraver, who prepared a popular set of engravings of Raphael's Cartoons in 1707 [23] Richard Westall (1765–1838), English painter of historical and rural subjects. His water-color drawings were distinguished in their time [24] Severn major river in Wales and western England [25] Paul and Virginia, a sentimental novel, published in 1786, by Bernardin de St. Pierre (1737–1814) Bridgewater, a city in Somersetshire [26] Frances Burney (Madame D'Arblay) (1752–1840), a popular English novelist Camilla, or a Picture of Youth was published in 1796

tenth of April, 1798, that I sat down to a volume of the
New Eloise, at the inn at Llangollen,[27] over a bottle of
sherry and a cold chicken. The letter I chose was St.
Preux's description of his feelings as he first caught a
glimpse from the heights of the Jura of the Pays de
Vaud, which I had brought with me as a *bonne bouche*[28]
to crown the evening with. It was my birth-day, and I
had for the first time come from a place in the neighbour-
hood to visit this delightful spot. The road to Llangollen
turns off between Chirk and Wrexham; and on passing
a certain point, you come all at once upon the valley,
which opens like an amphitheatre, broad, barren hills
rising in majestic state on either side, with "green up-
land swells that echo to the bleat of flocks" [29] below,
and the river Dee babbling over its stony bed in the midst
of them. The valley at this time "glittered green with
sunny showers," and a budding ash-tree dipped its tender
branches in the chiding stream. How proud, how glad I
was to walk along the high road that commanded the
delicious prospect, repeating the lines which I have just
quoted from Mr. Coleridge's poems! But besides the
prospect which opened beneath my feet, another also
opened to my inward sight, a heavenly vision, on which
were written, in letters large as Hope could make them,
these four words, LIBERTY, GENIUS, LOVE, VIR-
TUE; which have since faded into the light of common
day, or mock my idle gaze.

The beautiful is vanished, and returns not.[30]

---

[27] *New Eloise* Rousseau's most famous novel, published in 1761.
The setting of the novel is a village at the foot of the Alps
Llangollen is a town in Wales [28] *bonne bouche* a titbit or
sweetmeat taken after a meal, which leaves a pleasant taste in
one's mouth [29] Coleridge's "Ode to the Departing Year" (1796),
ll. 125–26. Hazlitt's next quotation is from the same poem
[30] **LIBERTY . . . returns not** the passage refers to Hazlitt's
early optimism about the revolutionary spirit of his age and his
subsequent disillusionment **into the light of common day**
Wordsworth's "Intimations Ode," l. 77 **The beautiful is
vanished, and returns not** Coleridge's *The Death of Wallenstein*, V, i, 68

Still I would return some time or other to this enchanted
spot; but I would return to it alone. What other self
could I find to share that influx of thoughts, of regret,
and delight, the traces of which I could hardly conjure
up to myself, so much have they been broken and de-
faced! I could stand on some tall rock, and overlook the
precipice of years that separates me from what I then
was. I was at that time going shortly to visit the poet
whom I have above named. Where is he now? Not only
I myself have changed—the world, which was then new
to me, has become old and incorrigible. Yet will I turn
to thee in thought, O sylvan Dee, as then thou wert in
joy, in youth and gladness; and thou shalt always be to
me the river of Paradise, where I will drink of the waters
of life freely!

There is hardly any thing that shews the short-sightedness or capriciousness of the imagination more than travelling does. With change of place we change our ideas,
nay, our opinions and feelings. We can by an effort indeed transport ourselves to old and long-forgotten scenes,
and then the picture of the mind revives again;[31] but
we forget those that we have just left. It seems that we
can think but of one place at a time. The canvas of the
fancy has only a certain extent, and if we paint one set
of objects upon it, they immediately efface every other.
We cannot enlarge our conceptions; we only shift our
point of view. The landscape bares its bosom to the en-
raptured eye; we take our fill of it; and seem as if we
could form no other image of beauty or grandeur. We
pass on, and think no more of it: the horizon that shuts
it from our sight also blots it from our memory, like a
dream. In travelling through a wild barren country, I
can form no idea of a woody and cultivated one. It appears to me that all the world must be barren, like what
I see of it. In the country we forget the town, and in
town we despise the country. "Beyond Hyde Park," says
Sir Fopling Flutter, "all is a desert." [32] All that part of

[31] **the picture . . . again** Wordsworth's "Tintern Abbey," l.
61   [32] George Etherege's comedy, *The Man of Mode or Sir
Fopling Flutter* (1676), V, ii. The line is spoken by the heroine
Harriet

the map that we do not see before us is a blank. The world in our conceit of it is not much bigger than a nutshell. It is not one prospect expanded into another, county joined to county, kingdom to kingdom, lands to seas, making an image voluminous and vast;—the mind can form no larger idea of space than the eye can take in at a single glance. The rest is a name written on a map, a calculation of arithmetic. For instance, what is the true signification of that immense mass of territory and population, known by the name of China to us? An inch of paste-board on a wooden globe, of no more account than a China orange! Things near us are seen of the size of life: things at a distance are diminished to the size of the understanding. We measure the universe by ourselves, and even comprehend the texture of our own being only piece-meal. In this way, however, we remember an infinity of things and places. The mind is like a mechanical instrument that plays a great variety of tunes, but it must play them in succession. One idea recalls another, but it at the same time excludes all others. In trying to renew old recollections, we cannot as it were unfold the whole web of our existence; we must pick out the single threads. So in coming to a place where we have formerly lived and with which we have intimate associations, every one must have found that the feeling grows more vivid the nearer we approach the spot, from the mere anticipation of the actual impression: we remember circumstances, feelings, persons, faces, names, that we had not thought of for years; but for the time all the rest of the world is forgotten!—To return to the question I have quitted above.

I have no objection to go to see ruins, aqueducts, pictures, in company with a friend or a party, but rather the contrary, for the former reason reversed. They are intelligible matters, and will bear talking about. The sentiment here is not tacit, but communicable and overt. Salisbury Plain is barren of criticism; but Stonehenge will bear a discussion antiquarian, picturesque, and philosophical. In setting out on a party of pleasure, the first consideration always is where we shall go: in taking a solitary ramble, the question is what we shall meet with by the way. The mind then is "its own place;"[33] nor are we anxious to arrive at the end of our journey. I can myself do the honours indifferently well to works of art and curiosity. I once took a party to Oxford with no mean *éclat*—shewed them that seat of the Muses at a distance,

> With glistering spires and pinnacles adorn'd—[34]

descanted on the learned air that breathes from the grassy quadrangles and stone-walls of halls and colleges—was at home in the Bodleian; and at Blenheim quite superseded the powdered Ciceroni[35] that attended us, and that pointed in vain with his wand to common-place beauties in matchless pictures.—As another exception to the above reasoning, I should not feel confident in venturing on a journey in a foreign country without a companion. I should want at intervals to hear the sound of my own language. There is an involuntary antipathy in the mind of an Englishman to foreign manners and notions, that requires the assistance of social sympathy to carry it off. As the distance from home increases, this relief, which was at first a luxury, becomes a passion and an appetite. A person would almost feel stifled to find himself in the deserts of Arabia without friends and countrymen: there must be allowed to be something in the view of Athens or old Rome, that claims the utterance of speech; and I own that the Pyramids are too mighty for any single contemplation. In such situations, so opposite to all one's ordinary train of ideas, one seems a species by one's-self, a limb torn off from society, unless one can meet with instant fellowship and support.—Yet I did not feel this want or craving very pressing once, when I first set my foot on the laughing shores of France. Calais was peopled with novelty and delight. The confused, busy murmur of the place was like oil and wine poured into my ears; nor did the mariners' hymn, which was sung from the top of an old crazy

---

[33] *Paradise Lost*, I, 254   [34] *éclat* brilliant effect or success   **With glistering . . . adorn'd"** *Paradise Lost*, III, 550   [35] **the Bodleian** library at Oxford, founded by **Sir Thomas Bodley** (1545–1613)   **Blenheim** palace of the Duke of Marlborough, near Oxford   **Ciceroni** guides

vessel in the harbour, as the sun went down, send an alien sound into my soul. I breathed the air of general humanity. I walked over "the vine-covered hills and gay regions of France," erect and satisfied; for the image of man was not cast down and chained to the foot of arbitrary thrones. I was at no loss for language, for that of all the great schools of painting was open to me.[36] The whole is vanished like a shade. Pictures, heroes, glory, freedom, all are fled: nothing remains but the Bourbons and the French people!—There is undoubtedly a sensation in travelling into foreign parts that is to be had nowhere else: but it is more pleasing at the time than lasting. It is too remote from our habitual associations to be a common topic of discourse or reference; and, like a dream or another state of existence, does not piece into our daily modes of life. It is an animated but a momentary hallucination. It demands an effort to exchange our actual for our ideal identity; and to feel the pulse of our old transports revive very keenly, we must "jump" all our present comforts and connexions. Our romantic and itinerant character is not to be domesticated. Dr. Johnson remarked how little foreign travel added to the facilities of conversation in those who had been abroad.[37] In fact, the time we have spent there is both delightful and in one sense instructive; but it appears to be cut out of our substantial, downright existence, and never to join kindly on to it. We are not the same, but another, and perhaps more enviable individual, all the time we are out of our own country. We are lost to ourselves, as well as to our friends. So the poet somewhat quaintly sings,

"Out of my country and myself I go."

Those who wish to forget painful thoughts, do well to absent themselves for a while from the ties and objects

[36] **Yet I did not feel this want . . . open to me** referring to Hazlitt's visit to France in 1802–3, in order to make copies of paintings in the Louvre **"the vine-covered hills and gay regions of France"** from "Song written for the purpose of being recited on the anniversary of the 14th August, 1791," by William Roscoe (P. P. Howe)   [37] **Dr. Johnson . . . abroad** Boswell's *Life of Johnson,* entry for May 13, 1778

that recall them: but we can be said only to fulfil our destiny in the place that gave us birth. I should on this account like well enough to spend the whole of my life in travelling abroad, if I could any where borrow another life to spend afterwards at home!

March, 1822   1825

The Fight

——"The *fight*, the *fight*'s the thing,
Wherein I'll catch the conscience of the king." [1]

Where there's a will, there's a way.— I said so to myself,
as I walked down Chancery-lane, about half-past six
o'clock on Monday the 10th of December,[2] to inquire at
Jack Randall's[3] where the fight the next day was to be;
and I found "the proverb" nothing "musty" [4] in the present instance. I was determined to see this fight, come what
would, and see it I did, in great style. It was my *first fight*,
yet it more than answered my expectations. Ladies! it is
to you I dedicate this description; nor let it seem out of
character for the fair to notice the exploits of the brave.
Courage and modesty are the old English virtues; and may
they never look cold and askance on one another! Think,
ye fairest of the fair, loveliest of the lovely kind, ye prac-
tisers of soft enchantment, how many more ye kill with
poisoned baits than ever fell in the ring; and listen with
subdued air and without shuddering, to a tale tragic only
in appearance, and sacred to the FANCY! [5]

I was going down Chancery-lane, thinking to ask at
Jack Randall's where the fight was to be, when looking
through the glass-door of the *Hole in the Wall*, I heard
a gentleman asking the same question *at* Mrs. Randall,
as the author of Waverley would express it.[6] Now Mrs.
Randall stood answering the gentleman's question, with

[1] Cf. *Hamlet*, II, ii, 633–34 [2] The year was 1821. The fight between Tom Hickman the Gas-man and Bill Neate occurred the
following day at Hungerford, Berkshire [3] "The Hole-in-the-
Wall," a London tavern maintained by **Jack Randall** (1794–
1828), a leading boxer between 1815 and 1821 [4] **"the proverb"**
. . . **"musty"** *Hamlet*, III, ii, 359 [5] **FANCY** nineteenth-cen-
tury word for the sport of boxing or its followers [6] **asking the
same question** *at* expression of the Scottish dialect **author of
Waverley** Sir Walter Scott

the authenticity of the lady of the Champion of the Light Weights. Thinks I, I'll wait till this person comes out, and learn from him how it is. For to say a truth, I was not fond of going into this house of call for heroes and phi- losophers, ever since the owner of it (for Jack is no gen- tleman) threatened once upon a time to kick me out of doors for wanting a mutton-chop at his hospitable board, when the conqueror in thirteen battles was more full of *blue ruin*[7] than of good manners. I was the more mortified at this repulse, inasmuch as I had heard Mr. James Simp- kins, hosier in the Strand, one day when the character of the *Hole in the Wall* was brought in question, observe— "The house is a very good house, and the company quite genteel: I have been there myself!" Remembering this un- kind treatment of mine host, to which mine hostess was also a party, and not wishing to put her in unquiet thoughts at a time jubilant like the present, I waited at the door, when, who should issue forth but my friend Jo. Toms,[8] and turning suddenly up Chancery-lane with that quick jerk and impatient stride which distinguishes a lover of the FANCY, I said, "I'll be hanged if that fellow is not going to the fight, and is on his way to get me to go with him." So it proved in effect, and we agreed to adjourn to my lodgings to discuss measures with that cordiality which makes old friends like new, and new friends like old, on great occasions. We are cold to others only when we are dull in ourselves, and have neither thoughts nor feel- ings to impart to them. Give a man a topic in his head, a throb of pleasure in his heart, and he will be glad to share it with the first person he meets. Toms and I, though we seldom meet, were an *alter idem*[9] on this memorable oc- casion, and had not an idea that we did not candidly im- part; and "so carelessly did we fleet the time," [10] that I wish no better, when there is another fight, than to have him for a companion on my journey down, and to return with my friend Jack Pigott,[11] talking of what was to hap-

[7] *blue ruin* cheap gin [8] *Jo. Toms* Joseph Parkes (1796–1865), at the time of the essay, a legal apprentice in London; subse- quently, a lawyer in Birmingham and a political figure of some importance [9] "a second self," "one and the same" [10] *As You Like It*, I, i, 124–25 [11] *Jack Pigott* P. G. Patmore (1786– 1855), close friend of Lamb and Hazlitt, journalist and minor writer

pen or of what did happen, with a noble subject always at hand, and liberty to digress to others whenever they offered. Indeed, on my repeating the lines from Spenser in an involuntary fit of enthusiasm,

> "What more felicity can fall to creature,
> Than to enjoy delight with liberty?" [12]

my last-named ingenious friend stopped me by saying that this, translated into the vulgate, meant "*Going to see a fight*."

Jo. Toms and I could not settle about the method of going down. He said there was a caravan, he understood, to start from Tom Belcher's[13] at two, which would go there *right out* and back again the next day. Now I never travel all night, and said I should get a cast to Newbury[14] by one of the mails. Jo. swore the thing was impossible, and I could only answer that I had made up my mind to it. In short, he seemed to me to waver, said he only came to see if I was going, had letters to write, a cause coming on the day after, and faintly said at parting (for I was bent on setting out that moment)—"Well, we meet at Philippi!" [15] I made the best of my way to Piccadilly. The mail coach stand was bare. "They are all gone," said I—"this is always the way with me—in the instant I lose the future—if I had not stayed to pour out that last cup of tea, I should have been just in time"—and cursing my folly and ill-luck together, without inquiring at the coach-office whether the mails were gone or not, I walked on in despite, and to punish my own dilatoriness and want of determination. At any rate, I would not turn back: I might get to Hounslow, or perhaps farther, to be on my road the next morning. I passed Hyde Park Corner (my Rubicon), and trusted to fortune. Suddenly I heard the clattering of a Brentford [16] stage, and the fight rushed full upon my fancy. I argued (not unwisely) that even a

[12] Spenser's *Muiopotmos* (1590), ll. 209–10 [13] "The Castle," a London tavern maintained by **Tom Belcher** (1783–1854), prize-fighter of some reputation, brother to the more famous boxer Jem Belcher [14] **Newbury** Berkshire town near Hungerford [15] Cf. *Julius Caesar*, IV, iii, 286 [16] **Brentford** suburban community west of London, in the general direction of Berkshire

Brentford coachman was better company than my own thoughts (such as they were just then), and at his invitation mounted the box with him. I immediately stated my case to him—namely, my quarrel with myself for missing the Bath or Bristol mail, and my determination to get on in consequence as well as I could, without any disparagement or insulting comparison between longer or shorter stages. It is a maxim with me that stage-coaches, and consequently stage-coachmen, are respectable in proportion to the distance they have to travel: so I said nothing on that subject to my Brentford friend. Any incipient tendency to an abstract proposition, or (as he might have construed it) to a personal reflection of this kind, was however nipped in the bud; for I had no sooner declared indignantly that I had missed the mails, than he flatly denied that they were gone along, and lo! at the instant three of them drove by in rapid, provoking, orderly succession, as if they would devour the ground before them. Here again I seemed in the contradictory situation of the man in Dryden who exclaims,

"I follow fate, which does too hard pursue!" [17]

If I had stopped to inquire at the White Horse Cellar, which would not have taken me a minute, I should now have been driving down the road in all the dignified unconcern and *ideal* perfection of mechanical conveyance. The Bath mail I had set my mind upon, and I had missed it, as I missed every thing else, by my own absurdity, in putting the will for the deed, and aiming at ends without employing means. "Sir," said he of the Brentford, "the Bath mail will be up presently, my brother-in-law drives it, and I will engage to stop him if there is a place empty." I almost doubted my good genius; but, sure enough, up it drove like lightning, and stopped directly at the call of the Brentford Jehu.[18] I would not have believed this possible, but the brother-in-law of a mail-coach driver is himself

[17] Dryden's heroic drama *The Indian Emperor* (1665), IV, iii
[18] **Jehu** proverbial name for wild driver, from the furious ride of Jehu, King of Israel, to Jezreel, to destroy the ruling house of the family of Ahab. 2 Kings, 9

no mean man. I was transferred without loss of time from the top of one coach to that of the other, desired the guard to pay my fare to the Brentford coachman for me as I had no change, was accommodated with a great coat, put up my umbrella to keep off a drizzling mist, and we began to cut through the air like an arrow. The mile-stones disappeared one after another, the rain kept off; Tom Turtle,[19] the trainer, sat before me on the coach-box, with whom I exchanged civilities as a gentleman going to the fight; the passion that had transported me an hour before was subdued to pensive regret and conjectural musing on the next day's battle; I was promised a place inside at Reading, and upon the whole, I thought myself a lucky fellow. Such is the force of imagination! On the outside of any other coach on the 10th of December with a Scotch mist drizzling through the cloudy moonlight air, I should have been cold, comfortless, impatient, and, no doubt, wet through; but seated on the Royal mail, I felt warm and comfortable, the air did me good, the ride did me good, I was pleased with the progress we had made, and confident that all would go well through the journey. When I got inside at Reading, I found Turtle and a stout valetudinarian, whose costume bespoke him one of the FANCY, and who had risen from a three months' sick bed to get into the mail to see the fight. They were intimate, and we fell into a lively discourse. My friend the trainer was confined in his topics to fighting dogs and men, to bears and badgers; beyond this he was "quite chap-fallen," [20] had not a word to throw at a dog, or indeed very wisely fell asleep, when any other game was started. The whole art of training (I, however, learnt from him,) consists in two things, exercise and abstinence, abstinence and exercise, repeated alternately and without end. A yolk of an egg with a spoonful of rum in it is the first thing in a morning, and then a walk of six miles till breakfast. This meal consists of a plentiful supply of tea and toast and beef-steaks. Then another six or seven miles till dinner-time, and another supply of solid beef or mutton with a pint of porter, and perhaps, at the utmost, a couple of

[19] **Tom Turtle** John Thurtell (1794–1824), amateur boxer and sportsman   [20] *Hamlet*, V, i, 212

glasses of sherry. Martin[21] trains on water, but this increases his infirmity on another very dangerous side. The Gas-man takes now and then a chirping glass (under the rose) to console him, during a six weeks' probation, for the absence of Mrs. Hickman—an agreeable woman, with (I understand) a pretty fortune of two hundred pounds. How matter presses on me! What stubborn things are facts! How inexhaustible is nature and art! "It is well," as I once heard Mr. Richmond [22] observe, "to see a variety." He was speaking of cock-fighting as an edifying spectacle. I cannot deny but that one learns more of what *is* (I do not say of what *ought to be*) in this desultory mode of practical study, than from reading the same book twice over, even though it should be a moral treatise. Where was I? I was sitting at dinner with the candidate for the honours of the ring, "where good digestion waits on appetite, and health on both." [23] Then follows an hour of social chat and native glee; and afterwards, to another breathing over heathy hill or dale. Back to supper, and then to bed, and up by six again—Our hero

> "Follows so the ever-running sun
> With profitable *ardour*—" [24]

to the day that brings him victory or defeat in the green fairy circle. Is not this life more sweet than mine? I was going to say; but I will not libel any life by comparing it to mine, which is (at the date of these presents) bitter as coloquintida and the dregs of aconitum! [25]

The invalid in the Bath mail soared a pitch above the

---

[21] **Jack Martin** (1796–1871), a boxer of some reputation between 1818 and 1821   [22] **Bill Richmond** (1763–1829), American Negro, who achieved considerable success as a boxer in England   [23] *Macbeth*, III, iv, 38–39   [24] Cf. *Henry V*, IV, i, 293–294   [25] At the time the essay was written (December, 1821 to January, 1822), Hazlitt was desperately in love with Sarah Walker, the flirtatious and slatternly daughter of Hazlitt's London landlord; and was arranging a trip to Scotland to obtain a divorce from his wife Sarah Stoddart Hazlitt   **bitter as coloquintida** *Othello*, I, iii, 356   **Coloquintida** and **aconitum** are, respectively, a bitter fruit used as a purgative drug, and a poisonous plant

trainer, and did not sleep so sound, because he had "more figures and more fantasies." [26] We talked the hours away merrily. He had faith in surgery, for he had had three ribs set right, that had been broken in a *turn-up*[27] at Belcher's, but thought physicians old women, for they had no antidote in their catalogue for brandy. An indigestion is an excellent common-place for two people that never met before. By way of ingratiating myself, I told him the story of my doctor, who, on my earnestly representing to him that I thought his regimen had done me harm, assured me that the whole pharmacopeia contained nothing comparable to the prescription he had given me; and, as a proof of its undoubted efficacy, said, that "he had had one gentleman with my complaint under his hands for the last fifteen years." This anecdote made my companion shake the rough sides of his three great coats with boisterous laughter; and Turtle, starting out of his sleep, swore he knew how the fight would go, for he had had a dream about it. Sure enough the rascal told us how the three first rounds went off, but "his dream," like others, "denoted a foregone conclusion." [28] He knew his men. The moon now rose in silver state, and I ventured, with some hesitation, to point out this object of placid beauty, with the blue serene beyond, to the man of science, to which his ear he "seriously inclined," [29] the more as it gave promise *d'un beau jour* for the morrow, and shewed the ring undrenched by envious showers, arrayed in sunny smiles. Just then, all going on well, I thought on my friend Toms, whom I had left behind, and said innocently, "There was a blockhead of a fellow I left in town, who said there was no possibility of getting down by the mail, and talked of going by a caravan from Belcher's at two in the morning, after he had written some letters." "Why," said he of the lapells, "I should not wonder if that was the very person we saw running about like mad from one coach-door to another, and asking if any one had seen a friend of his, a gentleman going to the fight, whom he had missed stu-

---

[26] Cf. *Julius Caesar*, II, i, 231 [27] *turn-up* a tussle or altercation
[28] "his dream . . . conclusion" *Othello*, III, iii, 427–28
[29] *Othello*, I, iii, 146

pidly enough by staying to write a note." "Pray Sir," said my fellow-traveller, "had he a plaid-cloak on?"—"Why, no," said I, "not at the time I left him, but he very well might afterwards, for he offered to lend me one." The plaid-cloak and the letter decided the thing. Joe, sure enough, was in the Bristol mail, which preceded us by about fifty yards. This was droll enough. We had now but a few miles to our place of destination, and the first thing I did on alighting at Newbury, both coaches stopping at the same time, was to call out, "Pray, is there a gentleman in that mail of the name of Toms?" "No," said Joe, borrowing something of the vein of Gilpin,[30] "for I have just got out." "Well!" says he, "this is lucky; but you don't know how vexed I was to miss you; for," added he, lowering his voice, "do you know when I left you I went to Belcher's to ask about the caravan, and Mrs. Belcher said very obligingly, she couldn't tell about that, but there were two gentlemen who had taken places by the mail and were gone on in a landau,[31] and she could frank us.[32] It's a pity I didn't meet with you; we could then have got down for nothing. But *mum's the word*." It's the devil for any one to tell me a secret, for it is sure to come out in print. I do not care so much to gratify a friend, but the public ear is too great a temptation to me.

Our present business was to get beds and a supper at an inn; but this was no easy task. The public-houses were full, and where you saw a light at a private house, and people poking their heads out of the casement to see what was going on, they instantly put them in and shut the window, the moment you seemed advancing with a suspicious overture for accommodation. Our guard and coachman thundered away at the outer gate of the Crown for some time without effect—such was the greater noise within;—and when the doors were unbarred, and we got admittance, we found a party assembled in the kitchen round a good hospitable fire, some sleeping, others drinking, others talking on politics and on the fight. A tall Eng-

[30] **the vein of Gilpin** a reference to the facetious humor of Cowper's "The Diverting History of John Gilpin" (1782)   [31] **landau** a four-wheeled carriage   [32] **frank us** secure us free passage

lish yeoman (something like Matthews[33] in the face, and quite as great a wag)—

"A lusty man to ben an abbot able,"—[34]

was making such a prodigious noise about rent and taxes, and the price of corn now and formerly, that he had prevented us from being heard at the gate. The first thing I heard him say was to a shuffling fellow who wanted to be off a bet for a shilling glass of brandy and water— "Confound it, man, don't be *insipid!*" Thinks I, that is a good phrase. It was a good omen. He kept it up so all night, nor flinched with the approach of morning. He was a fine fellow, with sense, wit, and spirit, a hearty body and a joyous mind, free-spoken, frank, convivial—one of that home English breed that went with Harry the Fifth to the siege of Harfleur—"standing like greyhounds on the slips," &c.[35] We ordered tea and eggs (beds were soon found to be out of the question) and this fellow's conversation was *sauce piquante*. It did one's heart good to see him brandish his oaken towel[36] and to hear him talk. He made mince-meat of a drunken, stupid, red-faced, quarrelsome, *frowsy* farmer, whose nose "he moralized into a thousand similes,"[37] making it out a firebrand like Bardolph's.[38] "I'll tell you what my friend," says he, "the landlady has only to keep you here to save fire and candle. If one was to touch your nose, it would go off like a piece of charcoal." At this the other only grinned like an idiot, the sole variety in his purple face being his little peering grey eyes and yellow teeth; called for another glass, swore he would not stand it; and after many attempts to provoke his humorous antagonist to single combat, which the other turned off (after working him up to a ludicrous pitch of choler) with great adroitness, he fell quietly asleep with a glass of liquor in his hand, which he could not lift to his head. His laughing persecutor made a speech over him,

[33] **Charles Matthews** (1776–1835), a leading comedian of the London stage   [34] Prologue to Chaucer's *Canterbury Tales*, l. 167   [35] *Henry V*, III, i, 31   [36] **oaken towel** slang phrase for stick or cudgel   [37] *As You Like It*, II, i, 44–45   [38] **Bardolph** companion of Falstaff, possessed of a large, inflamed nose ("an everlasting bonfire-light"). Cf. *Henry IV, Part I*, III, iii, 27–55

and turning to the opposite side of the room, where they were all sleeping in the midst of this "loud and furious fun," said, "There's a scene, by G-d, for Hogarth to paint. I think he and Shakspeare were our two best men at copying life!" This confirmed me in my good opinion of him. Hogarth, Shakspeare, and Nature, were just enough for him (indeed for any man) to know. I said, "You read Cobbett, don't you? At least," says I, "you talk just as well as he writes." He seemed to doubt this. But I said, "We have an hour to spare: if you'll get pen, ink, and paper, and keep on talking, I'll write down what you say; and if it doesn't make a capital Political Register, I'll forfeit my head. You have kept me alive to-night, however. I don't know what I should have done without you." He did not dislike this view of the thing, nor my asking if he was not about the size of Jem Belcher; and told me soon afterwards, in the confidence of friendship, that "the circumstance which had given him nearly the greatest concern in his life, was Cribb's beating Jem[39] after he had lost his eye by racket playing."—The morning dawns; that dim but yet clear light appears, which weighs like solid bars of metal on the sleepless eyelids; the guests drop down from their chambers one by one—but it was too late to think of going to bed now (the clock was on the stroke of seven), we had nothing for it but to find a barber's (the pole that glittered in the morning sun lighted us to his shop), and then a nine miles march to Hungerford. The day was fine, the sky was blue, the mists were retiring from the marshy ground, the path was tolerably dry, the sitting-up all night had not done us much harm—at least the cause was good; we talked of this and that with amicable difference, roving and sipping of many subjects, but still invariably we returned to the fight. At length, a mile to the left of Hungerford, on a gentle eminence, we saw the ring surrounded by covered carts, gigs, and carriages, of which hundreds had passed us on the road; Toms gave

[39] **Tom Cribb** (1781–1848), the Champion of England from 1809 until his retirement in 1822 **Jem Belcher** (1781–1811), the Champion of England from 1800 to 1805. Cribb defeated Belcher in celebrated matches in 1807 and 1809

a youthful shout, and we hastened down a narrow lane to the scene of action.

Reader, have you ever seen a fight? If not, you have a pleasure to come, at least if it is a fight like that between the Gas-man and Bill Neate. The crowd was very great when we arrived on the spot; open carriages were coming up, with streamers flying and music playing, and the country-people were pouring in over hedge and ditch in all directions, to see their hero beat or be beaten. The odds were still on Gas, but only about five to four. Gully[40] had been down to try Neate, and had backed him considerably, which was a damper to the sanguine confidence of the adverse party. About two hundred thousand pounds were pending. The Gas says, he has lost 3000*l*. which were promised him by different gentlemen if he had won. He had presumed too much on himself, which had made others presume on him. This spirited and formidable young fellow seems to have taken for his motto the old maxim, that "there are three things necessary to success in life—*Impudence! Impudence! Impudence!*" It is so in matters of opinion, but not in the *Fancy*, which is the most practical of all things, though even here confidence is half the battle, but only half. Our friend had vapoured and swaggered too much, as if he wanted to grin and bully his adversary out of the fight. "Alas! the Bristol man was not so tamed!" [41]—"This is *the grave-digger*" (would Tom Hickman exclaim in the moments of intoxication from gin and success, shewing his tremendous right hand), "this will send many of them to their long homes; I haven't done with them yet!" Why should he—though he had licked four of the best men within the hour, yet why should he threaten to inflict dishonourable chastisement on my old master Richmond, a veteran going off the stage, and who had borne his sable honours meekly? Magnanimity, my dear Tom, and bravery, should be inseparable. Or why should he go up to his antagonist, the first time he ever saw him at the Fives Court,[42] and measuring

[40] **John Gully** (1783–1863), the Champion of England in 1808
[41] Cf. Cowper's *Task*, II, 322. Bill Neate came from Bristol
[42] **Fives Court** important center for sports activities in London, where amateur boxing matches and professional exhibitions were held

him from head to foot with a glance of contempt, as Achilles surveyed Hector,[43] say to him—"What, are you Bill Neate? I'll knock more blood out of that great carcase of thine, this day fortnight, than you ever knock'd out of a bullock's!" It was not manly, 'twas not fighter-like. If he was sure of the victory (as he was not), the less said about it the better. Modesty should accompany the *Fancy* as its shadow. The best men were always the best behaved. Jem Belcher, the Game Chicken[44] (before whom the Gas-man could not have lived) were civil, silent men. So is Cribb, so is Tom Belcher, the most elegant of sparrers, and not a man for every one to take by the nose. I enlarged on this topic in the mail (while Turtle was asleep), and said very wisely (as I thought) that impertinence was a part of no profession. A boxer was bound to beat his man, but not to thrust his fist, either actually or by implication, in every one's face. Even a highwayman, in the way of trade, may blow out your brains, but if he uses foul language at the same time, I should say he was no gentleman. A boxer, I would infer, need not be a blackguard or a coxcomb, more than another. Perhaps I press this point too much on a fallen man —Mr. Thomas Hickman has by this time learnt that first of all lessons, "That man was made to mourn." [45] He has lost nothing by the late fight but his presumption; and that every man may do as well without! By an over-display of this quality, however, the public had been prejudiced against him, and the *knowing-ones* were taken in. Few but those who had bet on him wished Gas to win. With my own prepossessions on the subject, the result of the 11th of December appeared to me as fine a piece of poetical justice as I had ever witnessed. The difference of weight between the two combatants (14 stone to 12) was nothing to the sporting men. Great, heavy, clumsy, long-armed Bill Neate kicked the beam in the scale of the Gas-man's vanity. The amateurs were frightened at his big words, and thought they would make up for the difference

[43] **as Achilles surveyed Hector** Book XXII of the *Iliad* [44] **the Game Chicken** Henry Pearce (1777–1809), the Champion of England following his defeat of Jem Belcher in 1805 until his retirement in 1808 [45] title of a poem by Robert Burns

of six feet and five feet nine. Truly, the FANCY are not men of imagination. They judge of what has been, and cannot conceive of any thing that is to be. The Gas-man had won hitherto; therefore he must beat a man half as big again as himself—and that to a certainty. Besides, there are as many feuds, factions, prejudices, pedantic notions in the FANCY as in the state or in the schools. Mr. Gully is almost the only cool, sensible man among them, who exercises an unbiassed discretion, and is not a slave to his passions in these matters. But enough of reflections, and to our tale. The day, as I have said, was fine for a December morning. The grass was wet, and the ground miry, and ploughed up with multitudinous feet, except that, within the ring itself, there was a spot of virgin-green closed in and unprofaned by vulgar tread, that shone with dazzling brightness in the mid-day sun. For it was now noon, and we had an hour to wait. This is the trying time. It is then the heart sickens, as you think what the two champions are about, and how short a time will determine their fate. After the first blow is struck, there is no opportunity for nervous apprehensions; you are swallowed up in the immediate interest of the scene—but

> Between the acting of a dreadful thing
> And the first motion, all the interim is
> Like a phantasma, or a hideous dream.[46]

I found it so as I felt the sun's rays clinging to my back, and saw the white wintry clouds sink below the verge of the horizon. "So, I thought, my fairest hopes have faded from my sight!—so will the Gas-man's glory, or that of his adversary, vanish in an hour." The *swells* were parading in their white box-coats, the outer ring was cleared with some bruises on the heads and shins of the rustic assembly (for the *cockneys* had been distanced by the sixty-six miles); the time drew near, I had got a good stand; a bustle, a buzz, ran through the crowd, and, from the opposite side entered Neate, between his second and bottle-holder. He rolled along, swathed in his loose great coat, his knock-knees bending under his huge bulk; and, with a modest cheerful air, threw his hat into the ring. He then

[46] *Julius Caesar*, II, i, 63–65

just looked round, and began quietly to undress; when from the other side there was a similar rush and an opening made, and the Gas-man came forward with a conscious air of anticipated triumph, too much like the cock-of-the walk. He strutted about more than became a hero, sucked oranges with a supercilious air, and threw away the skin with a toss of his head, and went up and looked at Neate, which was an act of supererogation. The only sensible thing he did was, as he strode away from the modern Ajax, to fling out his arms, as if he wanted to try whether they would do their work that day. By this time they had stripped, and presented a strong contrast in appearance. If Neate was like Ajax, "with Atlantean shoulders, fit to bear" the pugilistic reputation of all Bristol, Hickman might be compared to Diomed,[47] light, vigorous, elastic, and his back glistened in the sun, as he moved about, like a panther's hide. There was now a dead pause—attention was awe-struck. Who at that moment, big with a great event, did not draw his breath short—did not feel his heart throb? All was ready. They tossed up for the sun, and the Gas-man won. They were led up to the *scratch*[48] —shook hands, and went at it.

In the first round every one thought it was all over. After making play a short time, the Gas-man flew at his adversary like a tiger, struck five blows in as many seconds, three first, and then following him as he staggered back, two more, right and left, and down he fell, a mighty ruin. There was a shout, and I said, "There is no standing this." Neate seemed like a lifeless lump of flesh and bone, round which the Gas-man's blows played with the rapidity of electricity or lightning, and you imagined he would only be lifted up to be knocked down again. It was as if Hickman held a sword or a fire in that right-hand of his, and directed it against an unarmed body. They met again, and Neate seemed, not cowed, but particularly cautious. I saw his teeth clenched together and his brows knit close against the sun. He held out both his arms at full length straight before him, like two sledge-hammers, and raised

---

[47] "with Atlantean shoulders, fit to bear" *Paradise Lost*, II, 306 **Ajax** and **Diomed** were famous opponents in the *Iliad*
[48] scratch "a line drawn across the ring, to which boxers are brought for an encounter" (*Oxford English Dictionary*)

his left an inch or two higher. The Gas-man could not get
over this guard—they struck mutually and fell, but without advantage on either side. It was the same in the next
round; but the balance of power was thus restored—the
fate of the battle was suspended. No one could tell how
it would end. This was the only moment in which opinion
was divided; for, in the next, the Gas-man aiming a mortal blow at his adversary's neck, with his right hand, and
failing from the length he had to reach, the other returned
it with his left at full swing, planted a tremendous blow
on his cheek-bone and eye-brow, and made a red ruin of
that side of his face. The Gas-man went down, and there
was another shout—a roar of triumph as the waves of
fortune rolled tumultuously from side to side. This was
a settler. Hickman got up, and "grinned horrible a ghastly
smile," [49] yet he was evidently dashed in his opinion of
himself; it was the first time he had ever been so punished;
all one side of his face was perfect scarlet, and his right eye
was closed in dingy blackness, as he advanced to the fight,
less confident, but still determined. After one or two
rounds, not receiving another such remembrancer, he ral-
lied and went at it with his former impetuosity. But in
vain. His strength had been weakened,—his blows could
not tell at such a distance,—he was obliged to fling himself at his adversary, and could not strike from his feet;
and almost as regularly as he flew at him with his right-
hand, Neate warded the blow, or drew back out of its
reach, and felled him with the return of his left. There
was little cautious sparring—no half-hits—no tapping and
trifling, none of the *petit-maîtreship*[50] of the art—they
were almost all knock-down blows:—the fight was a good
stand-up fight. The wonder was the half-minute time. If
there had been a minute or more allowed between each
round, it would have been intelligible how they should by
degrees recover strength and resolution; but to see two men
smashed to the ground, smeared with gore, stunned, senseless, the breath beaten out of their bodies; and then, before you recover from the shock, to see them rise up with
new strength and courage, stand ready to inflict or receive
mortal offence, and rush upon each other "like two clouds

[49] *Paradise Lost*, II, 846   [50] "effeminacy"

over the Caspian" [51]—this is the most astonishing thing of all:—this is the high and heroic state of man! From this time forward the event became more certain every round; and about the twelfth it seemed as if it must have been over. Hickman generally stood with his back to me; but in the scuffle, he had changed positions, and Neate just then made a tremendous lunge at him, and hit him full in the face. It was doubtful whether he would fall backwards or forwards; he hung suspended for a second or two, and then fell back, throwing his hands in the air, and with his face lifted up to the sky. I never saw any thing more terrific than his aspect just before he fell. All traces of life, of natural expression, were gone from him. His face was like a human skull, a death's head, spouting blood. The eyes were filled with blood, the nose streamed with blood, the mouth gaped blood. He was not like an actual man, but like a preternatural, spectral appearance, or like one of the figures in Dante's *Inferno.* Yet he fought on after this for several rounds, still striking the first desperate blow, and Neate standing on the defensive, and using the same cautious guard to the last, as if he had still all his work to do; and it was not till the Gas-man was so stunned in the seventeenth or eighteenth round, that his senses forsook him, and he could not come to time, that the battle was declared over.[52] Ye who despise the Fancy, do something to shew as much *pluck,* or as much self-possession as this, before you assume a superiority which you have never given a single proof of by any one action in the whole course of your lives!—When the Gas-man came to himself, the first words he uttered were, "Where am I? What is the matter?" "Nothing is the matter, Tom,—you

[51] Cf. *Paradise Lost,* II, 714–16 [52] "Scroggins said of the Gas-man, that he thought he was a man of that courage, that if his hands were cut off, he would still fight on with the stumps—like that of Widrington,—

——'In doleful dumps,
Who, when his legs were smitten off,
Still fought upon his stumps.' "

(Hazlitt's note) Scroggins, John Palmer ("Jack Scroggins") (1787–1836), a leading boxer between 1815 and 1820 Widrington a character in the ballad "Chevy Chase," from which Hazlitt quotes

have lost the battle, but you are the bravest man alive."
And Jackson[53] whispered to him, "I am collecting a purse
for you, Tom."—Vain sounds, and unheard at that moment! Neate instantly went up and shook him cordially
by the hand, and seeing some old acquaintance, began to
flourish with his fists, calling out, "Ah! you always said I
couldn't fight—What do you think now?" But all in good
humour, and without any appearance of arrogance; only
it was evident Bill Neate was pleased that he had won the
fight. When it was over, I asked Cribb if he did not think
it was a good one? He said, "*Pretty well!*" The carrier-
pigeons now mounted into the air, and one of them flew
with the news of her husband's victory to the bosom of
Mrs. Neate. Alas, for Mrs. Hickman!—

Mais au revoir, as Sir Fopling Flutter says. I went down
with Toms; I returned with Jack Pigott, whom I met on
the ground. Toms is a rattle-brain; Pigott is a sentimentalist. Now, under favour, I am a sentimentalist too—
therefore I say nothing, but that the interest of the excursion did not flag as I came back. Pigott and I marched
along the causeway leading from Hungerford to Newbury,
now observing the effect of a brilliant sun on the tawny
meads or moss-coloured cottages, now exulting in the fight,
now digressing to some topic of general and elegant literature. My friend was dressed in character for the occasion,
or like one of the FANCY; that is, with a double portion
of great coats, clogs, and overhauls: and just as we had
agreed with a couple of country-lads to carry his superfluous wearing-apparel to the next town, we were overtaken
by a return post-chaise, into which I got, Pigott preferring
a seat on the bar. There were two strangers already in the
chaise, and on their observing they supposed I had been
to the fight, I said I had, and concluded they had done
the same. They appeared, however, a little shy and sore on
the subject; and it was not till after several hints dropped,
and questions put, that it turned out that they had missed
it. One of these friends had undertaken to drive the other
there in his gig: they had set out, to make sure work, the

[53] **John Jackson** (1768–1845), Champion of England in 1795;
subsequently a teacher of boxing, numbering among his pupils
Byron and Hazlitt

day before at three in the afternoon. The owner of the
one-horse vehicle scorned to ask his way, and drove right
on to Bagshot, instead of turning off at Hounslow: there
they stopped all night, and set off the next day across the
country to Reading, from whence they took coach, and
got down within a mile or two of Hungerford, just half an
hour after the fight was over. This might be safely set
down as one of the miseries of human life. We parted
with these two gentlemen who had been to see the fight,
but had returned as they went, at Wolhampton, where we
were promised beds (an irresistible temptation, for Pigott
had passed the preceding night at Hungerford as we had
done at Newbury), and we turned into an old bow-win-
dowed parlour with a carpet and a snug fire; and after
devouring a quantity of tea, toast, and eggs, sat down to
consider, during an hour of philosophic leisure, what we
should have for supper. In the midst of an Epicurean de-
liberation between a roasted fowl and mutton-chops with
mashed potatoes, we were interrupted by an inroad of
Goths and Vandals—*O procul este profani*—not real
flash-men,[54] but interlopers, noisy pretenders, butchers
from Tothill-fields, brokers from Whitechapel,[55] who
called immediately for pipes and tobacco, hoping it would
not be disagreeable to the gentlemen, and began to insist
that it was *a cross*.[56] Pigott withdrew from the smoke and
noise into another room, and left me to dispute the point
with them for a couple of hours *sans intermission* by the
dial.[57] The next morning we rose refreshed; and on observing that Jack had a pocket volume in his hand, in which
he read in the intervals of our discourse, I inquired what
it was, and learned to my particular satisfaction that it
was a volume of the New Éloise. Ladies, after this, will
you contend that a love for the FANCY is incompatible
with the cultivation of sentiment?—We jogged on as before, my friend setting me up in a genteel drab great coat
and green silk handkerchief (which I must say became me

---

[54] **flash-men** patrons of the sport　[55] **Tothill-fields** and **Whitechapel** districts in London　[56] *a cross* slang phrase meaning "a
contest or match lost by collusory arrangement between the
principals" (*Oxford English Dictionary*)　[57] **couple of hours
. . . the dial** cf. *As You Like It*, II, vii, 32–33

exceedingly), and after stretching our legs for a few miles, and seeing Jack Randall, Ned Turner,[58] and Scroggins, pass on the top of one of the Bath coaches, we engaged with the driver of the second to take us to London for the usual fee. I got inside, and found three other passengers. One of them was an old gentleman with an aquiline nose, powdered hair, and a pigtail, and who looked as if he had played many a rubber at the Bath rooms. I said to myself, he is very like Mr. Windham;[59] I wish he would enter into conversation, that I might hear what fine observations would come from those finely-turned features. However, nothing passed, till, stopping to dine at Reading, some inquiry was made by the company about the fight, and I gave (as the reader may believe) an eloquent and animated description of it. When we got into the coach again, the old gentleman, after a graceful exordium, said, he had, when a boy, been to a fight between the famous Broughton[60] and George Stevenson, who was called the *Fighting Coachman*, in the year 1770, with the late Mr. Windham. This beginning flattered the spirit of prophecy within me, and he riveted my attention. He went on— "George Stevenson was coachman to a friend of my father's. He was an old man when I saw him some years afterwards. He took hold of his own arm and said, 'there was muscle here once, but now it is no more than this young gentleman's.' He added, 'well, no matter; I have been here long, I am willing to go hence, and hope I have done no more harm than another man.' Once," said my unknown companion, "I asked him if he had ever beat Broughton? He said Yes; that he had fought with him three times, and the last time he fairly beat him, though the world did not allow it. 'I'll tell you how it was, master. When the seconds lifted us up in the last round, we were so exhausted that neither of us could stand, and we fell upon one another, and as Master Broughton fell uppermost, the mob gave it in his favour, and he was said to

[58] **Ned Turner** (1791–1826), a leading boxer between 1817 and 1821   [59] **William Windham** (1750–1810), important statesman and member of parliament   [60] **John Broughton** (1705–89), perhaps the first professional English boxer, and author of the "Code" or rules of professional boxing that prevailed in England until 1838

have won the battle. But,' says he, 'the fact was, that as his second (John Cuthbert) lifted him up, he said to him, "I'll fight no more, I've had enough;" which,' says Stevenson, 'you know gave me the victory. And to prove to you that this was the case, when John Cuthbert was on his death-bed, and they asked him if there was any thing on his mind which he wished to confess, he answered, "Yes, that there was one thing he wished to set right, for that certainly Master Stevenson won that last fight with Master Broughton; for he whispered him as he lifted him up in the last round of all, that he had had enough." ' "This," said the Bath gentleman, "was a bit of human nature;" and I have written this account of the fight on purpose that it might not be lost to the world. He also stated as a proof of the candour of mind in this class of men, that Stevenson acknowledged that Broughton could have beat him in his best day; but that he (Broughton) was getting old in their last rencounter. When we stopped in Piccadilly, I wanted to ask the gentleman some questions about the late Mr. Windham, but had not courage. I got out, resigned my coat and green silk handkerchief to Pigott (loth to part with these ornaments of life), and walked home in high spirits.

P.S. Toms called upon me the next day, to ask me if I did not think the fight was a complete thing? I said I thought it was. I hope he will relish my account of it.

February, 1822

The Letter-Bell

Complaints are frequently made of the vanity and shortness of human life, when, if we examine its smallest details, they present a world by themselves. The most trifling objects, retraced with the eye of memory, assume the vividness, the delicacy, and importance of insects seen through a magnifying glass. There is no end of the brilliancy or the variety. The habitual feeling of the love of life may be compared to "one entire and perfect chrysolite," [1] which, if analysed, breaks into a thousand shining fragments. Ask the sum-total of the value of human life, and we are puzzled with the length of the account, and the multiplicity of items in it: take any one of them apart, and it is wonderful what matter for reflection will be found in it! As I write this, the *Letter-Bell* passes: it has a lively, pleasant sound with it, and not only fills the street with its importunate clamour, but rings clear through the length of many half-forgotten years. It strikes upon the ear, it vibrates to the brain, it wakes me from the dream of time, it flings me back upon my first entrance into life, and period of my first coming up to town, when all around was strange, uncertain, adverse—a hubbub of confused noises, a chaos of shifting objects—and when the sound alone, startling me with the recollection of a letter I had to send to the friends I had lately left, brought me as it were to myself, made me feel that I had links still connecting me with the universe, and gave me hope and patience to persevere. At that loud-tinkling, interrupted sound (now and then), the long line of blue hills near the place where I was brought up waves in the horizon, a golden sunset hovers over them, the dwarf-oaks rustle their red leaves in the evening-breeze, and the road from —— to ——, by which I first set out on my journey through life, stares me in the face as plain, but from time and change not less

[1] *Othello*, V, ii, 145

visionary and mysterious, than the pictures in the *Pilgrim's Progress*. I should notice, that at this time the light of the French Revolution circled my head like a glory, though dabbled with drops of crimson gore: I walked confident and cheerful by its side—

> "And by the vision splendid
> Was on my way attended." [2]

It rose then in the east: it has again risen in the west.[3] Two suns in one day, two triumphs of liberty in one age, is a miracle which I hope the Laureate will hail in appropriate verse. Or may not Mr. Wordsworth give a different turn to the fine passage, beginning—

> "What though the radiance which was once so
>   bright,
> Be now for ever vanished from my sight;
> Though nothing can bring back the hour
> Of glory in the grass, of splendour in the flower?" [4]

For is it not brought back, "like morn risen on *midnight*";[5] and may he not yet greet the yellow light shining on the evening bank with eyes of youth, of genius, and freedom, as of yore? [6] No, never! But what would not these persons give for the unbroken integrity of their early opinions—for one unshackled, uncontaminated strain—one *Io paean*[7] to Liberty—one burst of indignation against tyrants and sycophants, who subject other countries to slavery by force, and prepare their own for it by servile sophistry, as we see the huge serpent lick over its trembling, helpless victim with its slime and poison, before it devours it! On every stanza so penned should be written the word RECREANT! Every taunt,

---

[2] Wordsworth's "Intimations Ode," ll. 74–75 [3] **it has again risen in the west** refers to the Revolution of July, 1830, which overthrew the reactionary Bourbon monarch Charles X and put the "citizen king" Louis Philippe on the throne [4] "Intimations Ode," ll. 176–79 [5] Cf. *Paradise Lost*, V, 310–11 [6] **the yellow light . . . as of yore** refers to an incident during Hazlitt's first meeting with Wordsworth in 1798, as recorded in the essay "My First Acquaintance with Poets" (1823) [7] *Io paean* triumphant hymn of praise

every reproach, every note of exultation at restored light and freedom, would recal to them how their hearts failed them in the Valley of the Shadow of Death. And what shall we say to *him*—the sleep-walker, the dreamer, the sophist, the word-hunter, the craver after sympathy, but still vulnerable to truth, accessible to opinion, because not sordid or mechanical? The Bourbons being no longer tied about his neck, he may perhaps recover his original liberty of speculating; so that we may apply to him the lines about his own *Ancient Mariner*—

> "And from his neck so free
> The Albatross fell off, and sank
> Like lead into the sea." [8]

This is the reason I can write an article on the *Letter-Bell*, and other such subjects; I have never given the lie to my own soul. If I have felt any impression once, I feel it more strongly a second time; and I have no wish to revile and discard my best thoughts. There is at least a thorough *keeping*[9] in what I write—not a line that betrays a principle or disguises a feeling. If my wealth is small, it all goes to enrich the same heap; and trifles in this way accumulate to a tolerable sum. —Or if the Letter-Bell does not lead me a dance into the country, it fixes me in the thick of my town recollections, I know not how long ago. It was a kind of alarm to break off from my work when there happened to be company to dinner or when I was going to the play. *That* was going to the play, indeed, when I went twice a year, and had not been more than half a dozen times in my life. Even the idea that any one else in the house was going, was a sort of reflected enjoyment, and conjured up a lively anticipation of the scene. I remember a Miss D——, a maiden lady from Wales (who in her youth was to have been married to an earl), tantalized me greatly in this way, by talking all day of going to see Mrs. Siddons' "airs and graces" at night in some favourite part; and when the Letter-Bell announced that the time was approaching, and its last receding sound lingered on

[8] ll. 289–91   [9] *keeping* a term from painting, meaning the consistency and harmony of parts or colors in relation to the whole

the ear, or was lost in silence, how anxious and uneasy I became, lest she and her companion should not be in time to get good places—lest the curtain should draw up before they arrived—and lest I should lose one line or look in the intelligent report which I should hear the next morning! The punctuating of time at that early period—every thing that gives it an articulate voice—seems of the utmost consequence; for we do not know what scenes in the *ideal* world may run out of them: a world of interest may hang upon every instant, and we can hardly sustain the weight of future years which are contained in embryo in the most minute and inconsiderable passing events. How often have I put off writing a letter till it was too late! How often had to run after the postman with it—now missing, now recovering, the sound of his bell—breathless, angry with myself—then hearing the welcome sound come full round a corner—and seeing the scarlet costume which set all my fears and self-reproaches at rest! I do not recollect having ever repented giving a letter to the postman, or wishing to retrieve it after he had once deposited it in his bag. What I have once set my hand to, I take the consequences of, and have been always pretty much of the same humour in this respect. I am not like the person who, having sent off a letter to his mistress, who resided a hundred and twenty miles in the country, and disapproving, on second thoughts, of some expressions contained in it, took a post-chaise and four to follow and intercept it the next morning. At other times, I have sat and watched the decaying embers in a little *back* painting-room (just as the wintry day declined), and brooded over the half-finished copy of a Rembrandt, or a landscape by Vangoyen,[10] placing it where it might catch a dim gleam of light from the fire; while the Letter-Bell was the only sound that drew my thoughts to the world without, and reminded me that I had a task to perform in it. As to that landscape, methinks I see it now—

> "The slow canal, the yellow-blossomed vale,
> The willow-tufted bank, the gliding sail." [11]

[10] **Jan Van Goyen** (1596–1656), a leading Dutch landscape painter [11] Goldsmith's *Traveller* (1764), ll. 293–94

There was a windmill, too, with a poor low clay-built cottage beside it:—how delighted I was when I had made the tremulous, undulating reflection in the water, and saw the dull canvas become a lucid mirror of the commonest features of nature! Certainly, painting gives one a strong interest in nature and humanity (it is not the *dandy-school* of morals or sentiment)—

> "While with an eye made quiet by the power
> Of harmony and the deep power of joy,
> We see into the life of things." [12]

Perhaps there is no part of a painter's life (if we must tell "the secrets of the prison-house") [13] in which he has more enjoyment of himself and his art, than that in which after his work is over, and with furtive sidelong glances at what he has done, he is employed in washing his brushes and cleaning his pallet for the day. Afterwards, when he gets a servant in livery to do this for him, he may have other and more ostensible sources of satisfaction—greater splendour, wealth, or fame; but he will not be so wholly in his art, nor will his art have such a hold on him as when he was too poor to transfer its meanest drudgery to others—too humble to despise aught that had to do with the object of his glory and his pride, with that on which all his projects of ambition or pleasure were founded. "Entire affection scorneth nicer hands." [14] When the professor is above this mechanical part of his business, it may have become a *stalking-horse* [15] to other worldly schemes, but is no longer his *hobby-horse* and the delight of his inmost thoughts—

> "His shame in crowds, his solitary pride!" [16]

I used sometimes to hurry through this part of my occupation, while the Letter-Bell (which was my dinner-bell) summoned me to the fraternal board, where youth and hope

[12] Wordsworth's "Tintern Abbey," ll. 47–49 [13] *Hamlet*, I, v, 14 [14] *The Fairie Queene*, I, viii, 40 [15] *stalking-horse* term derived from hunting, referring to a horse, or the mechanical design of a horse, behind which the hunter hides in pursuing game; by extension, any means used to achieve some less than noble end [16] Goldsmith's *Deserted Village*, l. 412

"Made good digestion wait on appetite
And health on both"—[17]

or oftener I put it off till after dinner, that I might loiter longer and with more luxurious indolence over it, and connect it with the thoughts of my next day's labours.

The dustman's-bell, with its heavy, monotonous noise, and the brisk, lively tingle of the muffin-bell,[18] have something in them, but not much. They will bear dilating upon with the utmost license of inventive prose. All things are not alike *conductors* to the imagination. A learned Scotch professor found fault with an ingenious friend and arch-critic for cultivating a rookery on his grounds: the professor declared "he would as soon think of encouraging a *froggery*." This was barbarous as it was senseless. Strange, that a country that has produced the Scotch Novels and Gertrude of Wyoming[19] should want sentiment!

The postman's double-knock at the door the next morning is "more germain to the matter." [20] How that knock often goes to the heart! We distinguish to a nicety the arrival of the Two-penny or the General Post.[21] The summons of the latter is louder and heavier, as bringing news from a greater distance, and as, the longer it has been delayed, fraught with a deeper interest. We catch the sound of what is to be paid—eight-pence, nine-pence, a shilling—and our hopes generally rise with the postage. How we are provoked at the delay in getting change—at the servant who does not hear the door! Then if the postman passes, and we do not hear the expected knock, what a pang is there! It is like the silence of death—of hope! We think he does it on purpose, and enjoys all the misery of our suspense. I have sometimes walked out to see the Mail-Coach pass, by which I had sent a letter, or to meet it when I expected one. I never see a Mail-Coach, for this reason, but I look at it as the bearer of

[17] *Macbeth*, III, iv, 38–39 [18] **muffin-bell** used by sellers of muffins [19] **Scotch Novels** the novels of Sir Walter Scott **Gertrude of Wyoming** Thomas Campbell's popular romantic poem, published in 1809 [20] *Hamlet*, V, ii, 165 [21] **Two-penny** the postal service for mail within the London area **General Post** the postal service for mail in all parts of the British Isles beyond London

glad tidings—the messenger of fate. I have reason to say so.—The finest sight in the metropolis is that of the Mail-Coaches setting off from Piccadilly. The horses paw the ground, and are impatient to be gone, as if conscious of the precious burden they convey. There is a peculiar secrecy and despatch, significant and full of meaning, in all the proceedings concerning them. Even the outside passengers have an erect and supercilious air, as if proof against the accidents of the journey. In fact, it seems indifferent whether they are to encounter the summer's heat or winter's cold, since they are borne through the air in a winged chariot. The Mail-Carts drive up; the transfer of packages is made; and, at a signal given, they start off, bearing the irrevocable scrolls that give wings to thought, and that bind or sever hearts for ever. How we hate the Putney and Brentford [22] stages that draw up in a line after they are gone! Some persons think the sublimest object in nature is a ship launched on the bosom of the ocean: but give me, for my private satisfaction, the Mail-Coaches that pour down Piccadilly of an evening, tear up the pavement, and devour the way before them to the Land's-End!

In Cowper's time, Mail-Coaches were hardly set up;[23] but he has beautifully described the coming in of the Post-Boy:—

"Hark! 'tis the twanging horn o'er yonder bridge,
  That with its wearisome but needful length
  Bestrides the wintry flood, in which the moon
  Sees her unwrinkled face reflected bright:—
He comes, the herald of a noisy world,
  With spattered boots, strapped waist, and frozen
    looks;
News from all nations lumbering at his back.
True to his charge, the close-packed load behind,
Yet careless what he brings, his one concern
Is to conduct it to the destined inn;
And having dropped the expected bag, pass on.

[22] **Putney and Brentford** suburban communities to the west of London   [23] The first mail-coach service began in 1784. Previously, the mail was delivered by relays of horseback riders or "post-boys"

He whistles as he goes, light-hearted wretch!
Cold and yet cheerful; messenger of grief
Perhaps to thousands, and of joy to some;
To him indifferent whether grief or joy.
Houses in ashes and the fall of stocks,
Births, deaths, and marriages, epistles wet
With tears that trickled down the writer's cheeks
Fast as the periods from his fluent quill,
Or charged with amorous sighs of absent swains
Or nymphs responsive, equally affect
His horse and him, unconscious of them all." [24]

And yet, notwithstanding this, and so many other passages that seem like the very marrow of our being, Lord Byron denies that Cowper was a poet! [25]—The Mail-Coach is an improvement on the Post-Boy; but I fear it will hardly bear so poetical a description. The picturesque and dramatic do not keep pace with the useful and mechanical. The telegraphs that lately communicated the intelligence of the new revolution to all France within a few hours, are a wonderful contrivance; but they are less striking and appalling than the beacon-fires (mentioned by Æschylus),[26] which, lighted from hill-top to hill-top, announced the taking of Troy and the return of Agamemnon.

March, 1831

[24] *The Task*, IV, 1–22   [25] **Lord Byron . . . a poet!** refers to Byron's *Letter to* **** ******, *on the Rev. W. L. Bowles' Strictures on the Life and Writings of Pope* (1821), p. 47
[26] **beacon-fires . . . Æschylus** described in the opening scenes of his play *Agamemnon*

A Farewell to Essay-Writing

"This life is best, if quiet life is best." [1]

Food, warmth, sleep, and a book; these are all I at present ask—the *ultima thule*[2] of my wandering desires. Do you not then wish for

"A friend in your retreat,
Whom you may whisper, solitude is sweet?" [3]

Expected, well enough:—gone, still better. Such attractions are strengthened by distance. Nor a mistress? "Beautiful mask! I know thee!" When I can judge of the heart from the face, of the thoughts from the lips, I may again trust myself. Instead of these, give me the robin red-breast, pecking the crumbs at the door, or warbling on the leafless spray, the same glancing form that has followed me wherever I have been, and "done its spiriting gently";[4] or the rich notes of the thrush that startle the ear of winter, and seem to have drunk up the full draught of joy from the very sense of contrast. To these I adhere and am faithful, for they are true to me; and, dear in themselves, are dearer for the sake of what is departed, leading me back (by the hand) to that dreaming world, in the innocence of which they sat and made sweet music, waking the promise of future years, and answered by the eager throbbings of my own breast. But now "the credulous hope of mutual minds is o'er," [5] and I turn back from the world that has deceived me, to nature that lent

[1] *Cymbeline*, III, iii, 29–30 [2] *ultima thule* the final point or ultimate achievement; originally, the ancient designation for an island far north of England, believed to be the extreme limit of the earth [3] Cowper's "Retirement" (1782), ll. 741–42 [4] *The Tempest*, I, ii, 298 [5] Byron's *Don Juan*, I, ccxvi

it a false beauty, and that keeps up the illusion of the past. As I quaff my libations of tea in a morning, I love to watch the clouds sailing from the west, and fancy that "the spring comes slowly up this way." [6] In this hope, while "fields are dank and ways are mire," [7] I follow the same direction to a neighbouring wood, where, having gained the dry, level greensward, I can see my way for a mile before me, closed in on each side by copse-wood, and ending in a point of light more or less brilliant, as the day is bright or cloudy. What a walk is this to me! I have no need of book or companion—the days, the hours, the thoughts of my youth are at my side, and blend with the air that fans my cheek. Here I can saunter for hours, bending my eye forward, stopping and turning to look back, thinking to strike off into some less trodden path, yet hesitating to quit the one I am in, afraid to snap the brittle threads of memory. I remark the shining trunks and slender branches of the birch-trees, waving in the idle breeze; or a pheasant springs up on whirring wing; or I recall the spot where I once found a wood-pigeon at the foot of a tree, weltering in its gore, and think how many seasons have flown since "it left its little life in air." Dates, names, faces come back—to what purpose? Or why think of them now? Or rather, why not think of them oftener? We walk through life, as through a narrow path, with a thin curtain drawn around it; behind are ranged rich portraits, airy harps are strung—yet we will not stretch forth our hands and lift aside the veil, to catch glimpses of the one, or sweep the chords of the other. As in a theatre, when the old-fashioned green curtain drew up, groups of figures, fantastic dresses, laughing faces, rich banquets, stately columns, gleaming vistas appeared beyond; so we have only at any time to "peep through the blanket of the past," [8] to possess ourselves at once of all that has regaled our senses, that is stored up in our memory, that has struck our fancy, that has pierced our hearts:—yet to all this we are indifferent, insensible, and seem intent only on the present vexation, the future disappointment. If there is a Titian hanging up in the room

[6] Coleridge's *Christabel*, l. 22 [7] Milton's "Sonnet XX (To Mr. Lawrence)," l. 2 [8] *Macbeth*, I, v, 54

with me, I scarcely regard it: how then should I be expected to strain the mental eye so far, or to throw down, by the magic spells of the will, the stone-walls that enclose it in the Louvre? There is one head there, of which I have often thought, when looking at it, that nothing should ever disturb me again, and I would become the character it represents—such perfect calmness and self-possession reigns in it! Why do I not hang an image of this in some dusky corner of my brain, and turn an eye upon it ever and anon, as I have need of some such talisman to calm my troubled thoughts? The attempt is fruitless, if not natural; or, like that of the French, to hang garlands on the grave, and to conjure back the dead by miniature-pictures of them while living! It is only some actual coincidence, or local association that tends, without violence, to "open all the cells where memory slept." [9] I can easily, by stooping over the long-sprent grass and clay-cold clod, recall the tufts of primroses, or purple hyacinths, that formerly grew on the same spot, and cover the bushes with leaves and singing-birds, as they were eighteen summers ago;[10] or prolonging my walk and hearing the sighing gale rustle through a tall, strait wood at the end of it, can fancy that I distinguish the cry of hounds, and the fatal group issuing from it, as in the tale of Theodore and Honoria.[11] A moaning gust of wind aids the belief; I look once more to see whether the trees before me answer to the idea of the horror-stricken grove, and an air-built city towers over their grey tops.

"Of all the cities in Rumanian lands.
The chief and most renown'd Ravenna stands." [12]

[9] Cowper's *The Task*, VI, 11–12 [10] **eighteen summers ago** this essay was written at Winterslow, Wiltshire, where Hazlitt's first wife owned property. He first lived there following his marriage in 1808, and it remained a rural retreat until the end of his life [11] **Theodore and Honoria** a tale from Boccaccio's *Decameron*, translated by Dryden in his *Fables Ancient and Modern* (1700). The tale involves the horrifying appearance in a dense thicket of a pair of lovers from hell, who live out their eternity with the maiden being pursued and hideously attacked by the suitor and his hounds [12] The opening lines of Dryden's translation

I return home resolved to read the entire poem through, and, after dinner, drawing my chair to the fire, and holding a small print close to my eyes, launch into the full tide of Dryden's couplets (a stream of sound), comparing his didactic and descriptive pomp with the simple pathos and picturesque truth of Boccacio's story, and tasting with a pleasure, which none but an habitual reader can feel, some quaint examples pronunciation in this accomplished versifier.

> "Which when Honoria view'd,
> The fresh *impulse* her former fright renew'd."
> *Theodore and Honoria.*[13]

"And made th'*insult*, which in his grief appears,
> The means to mourn thee with my pious tears.
> *Sigismonda and Guiscardo.*" [14]

These trifling instances of the wavering and unsettled state of the language give double effect to the firm and stately march of the verse, and make me dwell with a sort of tender interest on the difficulties and doubts of an earlier period of literature. They pronounced words then in a manner which we should laugh at now; and they wrote verse in a manner which we can do anything but laugh at. The pride of a new acquisition seems to give fresh confidence to it; to impel the rolling syllables through the moulds provided for them, and to overflow the envious bounds of rhyme into time-honoured triplets. I am much pleased with Leigh Hunt's mention[15] of Moore's involuntary admiration of Dryden's free, unshackled verse, and of his repeating *con amore*, and with an Irish spirit and accent, the fine lines—

> "Let honour and preferment go for gold,
> But glorious beauty isn't to be sold!" [16]

[13] ll. 342–43   [14] ll. 668–69 of another tale from Boccaccio translated by Dryden   [15] **Leigh Hunt's mention** in Leigh Hunt's *Lord Byron and Some of his Contemporaries* (1828), an ill-tempered account of Byron, with essays on Shelley, Keats, Coleridge, and other contemporaries. An essay critical of Hazlitt's character was written for the volume, but withdrawn before publication   [16] Dryden's Epilogue to Nathaniel Lee's tragedy *Mithridates, King of Pontus* (1678), ll. 16–17

What sometimes surprises me in looking back to the past, is, with the exception already stated, to find myself so little changed in the time. The same images and trains of thought stick by me: I have the same tastes, likings, sentiments, and wishes that I had then. One great ground of confidence and support has, indeed, been struck from under my feet; but I have made it up to myself by proportionable pertinacity of opinion. The success of the great cause, to which I had vowed myself, was to me more than all the world: I had a strength in its strength, a resource which I knew not of, till it failed me for the second time.[17]

> "Fall'n was Glenartny's stately tree!
> Oh! ne'er to see Lord Ronald more!" [18]

It was not till I saw the axe laid to the root, that I found the full extent of what I had to lose and suffer. But my conviction of the right was only established by the triumph of the wrong; and my earliest hopes will be my last regrets. One source of this unbendingness, (which some may call obstinacy,) is that, though living much alone, I have never worshipped the Echo. I see plainly enough that black is not white, that the grass is green, that kings are not their subjects; and, in such self-evident cases, do not think it necessary to collate my opinions with the received prejudices. In subtler questions, and matters that admit of doubt, as I do not impose my opinion on others without a reason, so I will not give up mine to them without a better reason; and a person calling me names, or giving himself airs of authority, does not convince me of his having taken more pains to find out the truth than I have, but the contrary. Mr. Gifford [19] once said, that "while I was sitting over my gin and tobacco-pipes, I fancied myself a Leibnitz." He did not so much as know that I had ever read a metaphysical book:—was I therefore, out of complaisance or deference to him, to forget whether I had or not? I am rather disappointed, both on my own account and his, that Mr.

[17] **the second time** the defeat of Napoleon at Waterloo (1815)
[18] Scott's ballad "Glenfinlas" (1801)   [19] **William Gifford** (1756–1826), editor of the Tory publication, *The Quarterly Review,* extremely hostile to the literary and political opinions of Hazlitt

Hunt has missed the opportunity of explaining the character of a friend, as clearly as he might have done. He is puzzled to reconcile the shyness of my pretensions, with the inveteracy and sturdiness of my principles. I should have thought they were nearly the same thing. Both from disposition and habit, I can *assume* nothing in word, look, or manner. I cannot steal a march upon public opinion in any way. My standing upright, speaking loud, entering a room gracefully, proves nothing; therefore I neglect these ordinary means of recommending myself to the good graces and admiration of strangers, (and, as it appears, even of philosophers and friends). Why? Because I have other resources, or, at least, am absorbed in other studies and pursuits. Suppose this absorption to be extreme, and even morbid, that I have brooded over an idea till it has become a kind of substance in my brain, that I have reasons for a thing which I have found out with much labour and pains, and to which I can scarcely do justice without the utmost violence of exertion, (and that only to a few persons,)—is this the reason for my playing off my out-of-the-way notions in all companies, wearing a prim and self-complacent air, as if I were "the admired of all observers?" [20] or is it not rather an argument, (together with a want of animal spirits,) why I should retire into myself, and perhaps acquire a nervous and uneasy look, from a consciousness of the disproportion between the interest and conviction I feel on certain subjects, and my ability to communicate what weighs upon my own mind to others? If my ideas, which I do not avouch, but suppose, lie below the surface, why am I to be always attempting to dazzle superficial people with them, or smiling, delighted, at my own want of success?

What I have here stated is only the excess of the common and well-known English and scholastic character. I am neither a buffoon, a fop, nor a Frenchman, which Mr. Hunt would have me to be. He finds it odd that I am a close reasoner and a loose dresser. I have been (among other follies) a hard liver as well as a hard thinker; and the consequences of that will not allow me to dress as I please. People in real life are not like players on a stage, who put on a certain look or *costume*, merely for effect.

[20] Cf. *Hamlet*, III, i, 162

I am aware, indeed, that the gay and airy pen of the author does not seriously probe the errors or misfortunes of his friends—he only glances at their seeming peculiarities, so as to make them odd and ridiculous; for which forbearance few of them will thank him. Why does he assert that I was vain of my hair when it was black, and am equally vain of it now it is grey, when this is true in neither case? This transposition of motives makes me almost doubt whether Lord Byron was thinking so much of the rings on his fingers[21] as his biographer was. These sorts of criticisms should be left to women. I am made to wear a little hat, stuck on the top of my head, the wrong way. Nay, I commonly wear a large slouching hat over my eyebrows; and if ever I had another, I must have twisted it about in any shape to get rid of the annoyance. This probably tickled Mr. Hunt's fancy, and retains possession of it, to the exclusion of the obvious truism, that I naturally wear "a melancholy hat."

I am charged with using strange gestures and contortions of features in argument, in order to "look energetic." One would rather suppose that the heat of the argument produced the extravagance of the gestures, as I am said to be calm at other times. It is like saying that a man in a passion clenches his teeth, not because he is, but in order to seem, angry. Why should everything be construed into air and affectation? With Hamlet, I may say, "I know not *seems*." [22]

Again, my old friend and pleasant "Companion" remarks it, as an anomaly in my character, that I crawl about the Fives-Court like a cripple till I get the racket in my hand, when I start up as if I was possessed with a devil. I have then a motive for exertion; I lie by for difficulties and extreme cases. *Aut Caesar aut nullus.*[23] I have no notion of doing nothing with an air of importance, nor should I ever take a liking to the game of battledoor and shuttlecock.—I have only seen by accident a page of the unpublished Manuscript relating to the present subject, which I dare say is, on the whole, friendly and just, and

[21] **Lord Byron . . . fingers** Evidence of Byron's vanity and effeminacy of character offered in Hunt's *Lord Byron and Some of his Contemporaries* [22] *Hamlet*, I, ii, 76 [23] "Either Caesar or no one"

which has been suppressed as being too favourable, considering certain prejudices against me.

In matters of taste and feeling, one proof that my conclusions have not been quite shallow or hasty, is the circumstance of their having been lasting. I have the same favourite books, pictures, passages, that I ever had: I may therefore presume that they will last me my life—nay, I may indulge a hope that my thoughts will survive me. This continuity of impression is the only thing on which I pride myself. Even L——,[24] whose relish of certain things is as keen and earnest as possible, takes a surfeit of admiration, and I should be afraid to ask about his select authors or particular friends, after a lapse of ten years. As to myself, any one knows where to have me. What I have once made up my mind to, I abide by to the end of the chapter. One cause of my independence of opinion is, I believe, the liberty I give to others, or the very diffidence and distrust of making converts. I should be an excellent man on a jury: I might say little, but should starve "the other eleven obstinate fellows" out. I remember Mr. Godwin writing to Mr. Wordsworth, that "his tragedy of Antonio could not fail of success." It was damned past all redemption.[25] I said to Mr. Wordsworth that I thought this a natural consequence; for how could any one have a dramatic turn of mind who judged entirely of others from himself? Mr. Godwin might be convinced of the excellence of his work; but how could he know that others would be convinced of it, unless by supposing that they were as wise as himself, and as infallible critics of dramatic poetry—so many Aristotles sitting in judgment on Euripides! This shows why pride is connected with shyness and reserve; for the really proud have not so high an opinion of the generality as to suppose that they can understand them, or that there is any common measure between them. So Dryden exclaims of his opponents with bitter disdain—

"Nor can I think what thoughts they can conceive." [26]

I have not sought to make partisans, still less did I dream of making enemies; and have therefore kept my opinions

[24] Lamb   [25] Godwin's *Antonio* was produced in London in 1800
[26] Dryden's *Hind and the Panther*, I, 315

myself, whether they were currently adopted or not. To get others to come into our ways of thinking, we must go over to theirs; and it is necessary to follow, in order to lead. At the time I lived here formerly, I had no suspicion that I should ever become a voluminous writer; yet I had just the same confidence in my feelings before I had ventured to air them in public as I have now. Neither the outcry *for* or *against* moves me a jot: I do not say that the one is not more agreeable than the other.

Not far from the spot where I write, I first read Chaucer's *Flower and Leaf*,[27] and was charmed with that young beauty, shrouded in her bower, and listening with ever-fresh delight to the repeated song of the nightingale close by her—the impression of the scene, the vernal landscape, the cool of the morning, the gushing notes of the songstress,

"And ayen, methought she sung close by mine ear,"

is as vivid as if it had been of yesterday; and nothing can persuade me that that is not a fine poem. I do not find this impression conveyed in Dryden's version, and therefore nothing can persuade me that that is as fine. I used to walk out at this time with Mr. and Miss L——[28] of an evening, to look at the Claude Lorraine skies over our heads, melting from azure into purple and gold, and to gather mushrooms, that sprung up at our feet, to throw into our hashed mutton at supper. I was at that time an enthusiastic admirer of Claude, and could dwell for ever on one or two of the finest prints from him hung round my little room; the fleecy flocks, the bending trees, the winding streams, the groves, the nodding temples, the air-wove hills, and distant sunny vales; and tried to translate them into their lovely living hues. People then told me that Wilson[29] was much superior to Claude. I did not believe them. Their pictures have since been seen together at the British Institution,[30] and all the

[27] *Flower and Leaf* an allegorical poem no longer attributed to Chaucer. Dryden included a "translation" of it in his *Fables Ancient and Modern*   [28] Charles and Mary Lamb   [29] **Richard Wilson** (1713?–82), English landscape painter of some reputation in the early nineteenth century   [30] **British Institution** founded in 1805–6 for the encouragement of the fine arts in England

world have come into my opinion. I have not, on that
account, given it up. I will not compare our hashed
mutton with Amelia's;[31] but it put us in mind of it, and
led to a discussion, sharply seasoned and well sustained,
till midnight, the result of which appeared some years
after in the Edinburgh Review.[32] Have I a better opinion
of those criticisms on that account, or should I therefore
maintain them with greater vehemence and tenaciousness?
Oh no! Both rather with less, now that they are before
the public, and it is for them to make their election.

It is in looking back to such scenes that I draw my
best consolation for the future. Later impressions come
and go, and serve to fill up the intervals; but these are
my standing resource, my true classics. If I have had few
real pleasures or advantages, my ideas, from their sinewy
texture, have been to me in the nature of realities; and
if I should not be able to add to the stock, I can live by
husbanding the interest. As to my speculations, there is
little to admire in them but my admiration of others; and
whether they have an echo in time to come or not, I have
learnt to set a grateful value on the past, and am content to wind up the account of what is personal only to
myself and the immediate circle of objects in which I
have moved, with an act of easy oblivion,

>"And curtain close such scene from every future
>   view." [33]

March, 1828

---

[31] **Amelia's** an affecting scene in Book X, Chapter v, of Fielding's novel *Amelia* (1751), in which the long-suffering heroine
delays her dinner and finally eats alone, while her husband drinks
and gambles at a tavern   [32] **Edinburgh Review** refers to Hazlitt's essay "Standard Novels and Romances," published in February, 1815   [33] William Collins' "Ode on the Poetical Character" (1746), l. 76

bibliography

editions

The Complete Works of William Hazlitt, 21 vols., P. P. Howe, ed. (London, 1930–34).

Keynes, Geoffrey, *Bibliography of William Hazlitt* (London, 1931).

Wilcox, Stewart C., *Hazlitt in the Workshop: The Manuscript of "The Fight"* (Baltimore, 1943).

biography

Howe, P. P., *The Life of William Hazlitt* (London, 1947).

criticism

Albrecht, W. P., *Hazlitt and the Creative Imagination* (Lawrence, Kan., 1965).

Baker, Herschel, *William Hazlitt* (Cambridge, Mass., 1962).

Bullitt, John M., "Hazlitt and the Romantic Conception of the Imagination," *Philological Quarterly*, XXIV (1945), 343–61.

O'Hara, J. D., "Hazlitt and the Functions of the Imagination," PMLA, LXXXI (1966), 552–62.

Schneider, Elizabeth, "Hazlitt," in *The English Romantic Poets and Essayists: A Review of Research and Criticism*, Carolyn W. Houtchens and Lawrence H. Houtchens, eds. (New York, 1957).

Woolf, Virginia, "William Hazlitt," in *The Common Reader*, Second Series (London, 1932).